THE
PLANAR HEAD
WORKBOOK
by Robert Bissett

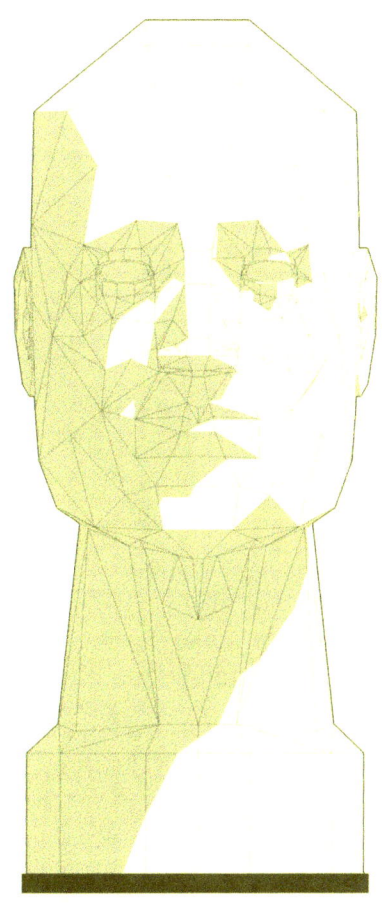

BUILD A LIFE-SIZE HUMAN HEAD

Complete Plans and Instructions

for teachers

students

artists

photographers

sculptors

crafters

jewelers

decorators

and others.

The Planar Head Workbook
CreatSpace/Amazon

Naples, Idaho 83847

Copyright 2012 by Robert Bissett

All rights reserved.

ISBN-13: 978-1475050639

ISBN-10: 1475050631

Cover
Design by Robert Bissett
Cover Art: Loi at the Festival
by Robert Bissett

Interior
All text, photos, drawings
by Robert Bissett

Dedication: To Loi,

Sine Qua Non

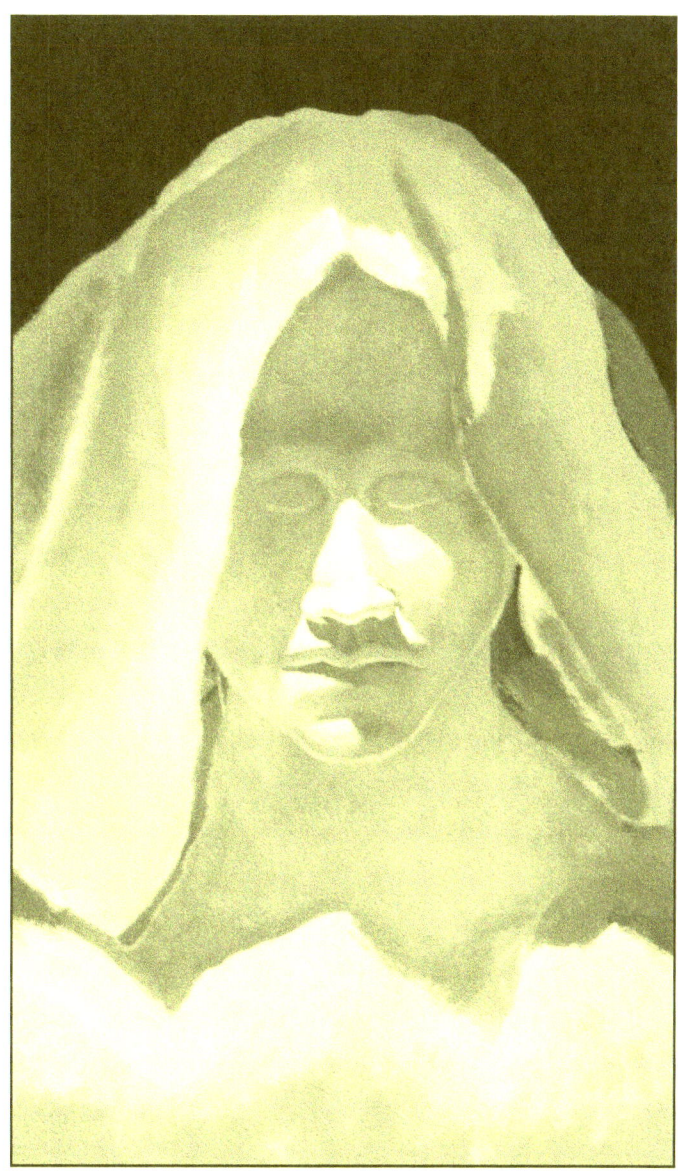

Painting from a paper mache bust of Loi.

CONTENTS

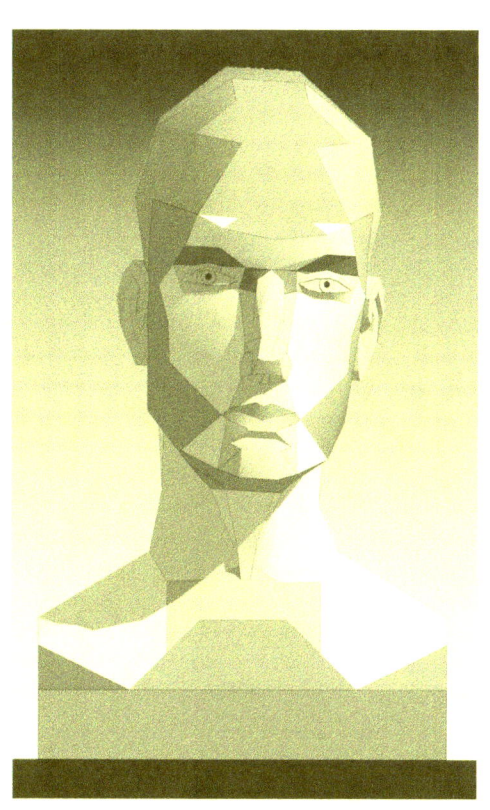

FORWARD

Have you ever wanted to draw or paint the human head? If you have tried it you probably have already discovered that faces are just about the most difficult thing there is to do. Proportions and perspective have to be right. You want to get a likeness with the right expression. The slightest pencil mark or brush stroke can make an amazing difference. How do you reach this high level of skill ?

Working from life is the best way. Photos are fine for reference, but you need to develop a feel for the three dimensional form. So, find a friend or family member who is willing and able to sit perfectly still for hours at a time and get started practicing! Can't think of anyone? Ok, hire a professional model. You'd soon go broke unless you are part of the 1%.

The traditional path to portrait success starts with working from plaster casts for obvious reasons. Even better is to begin with a planar head…the human head broken up into planes which simplifies the task of converting a 3D object to a 2D surface. Planar heads are available commercially and can be ordered online. However, you would be well advised to make your own for two reasons: 1) cost and 2) feel. Of the two 'feel' is the most important. The experience of forming and building a three dimensional human head with your own hands is invaluable. By making your own model, shaping it with your own fingers, you will internalize the forms. They will become fixed in your mind never to be forgotten.

The purpose of this book is to provide you with an easy and inexpensive way to make your own model of a life-sized human head. Useful for teachers, students, artists, photographers, sculptors, hobbyist, crafters, jewelers, decorators and others.

How I did it and why.

An in depth search on the internet for a 3D digital planar head came up with nothing. I decided to make one myself using Google Sketchup. I used only the basic tools found in the free version building it one line and one plane at a time. Organic modeling plugins are available, but they would result in a great many tiny planes. The idea was to model a useable head with the minimum number of planes. I divided the head into sections and unfolded them with the free unfold plugin. After going through the process I thought I could make a better head which resulted in Planar Head Two found in Part 5.

PART 1

What you'll need...

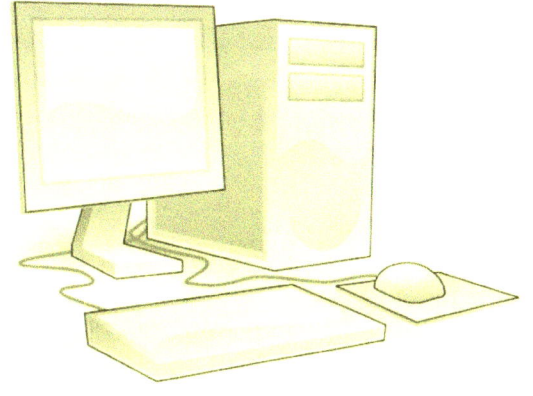

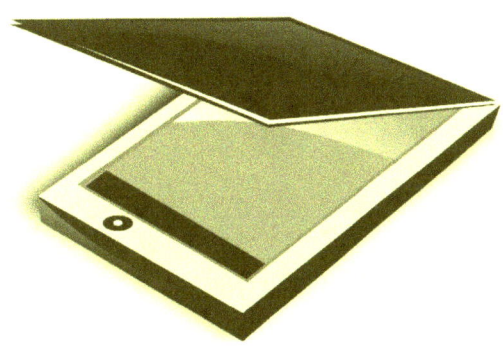

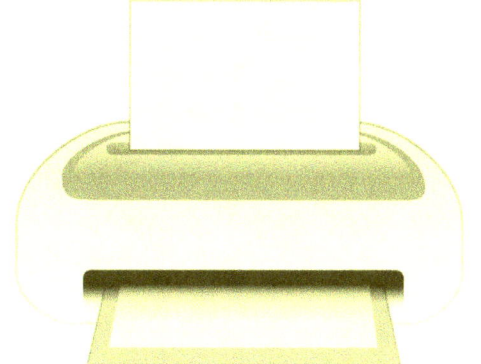

and cover stock.

...or
A Copy Machine...or Tracing Paper and Pencil
and Transfer paper onto cardboard.

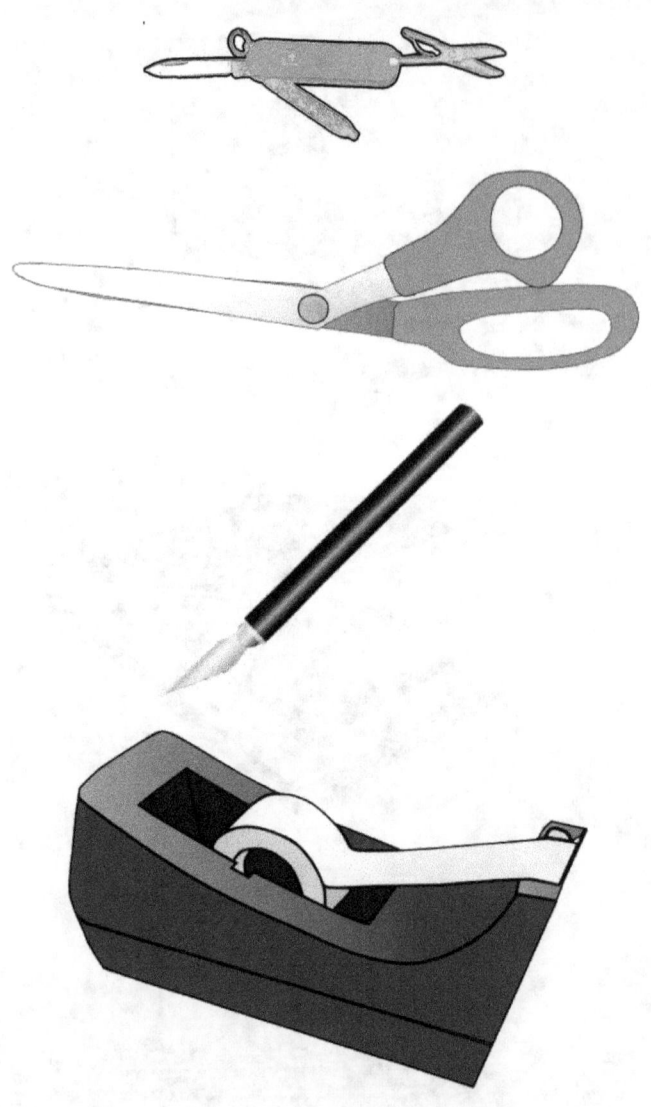

PART 2

MAIN VIEWS

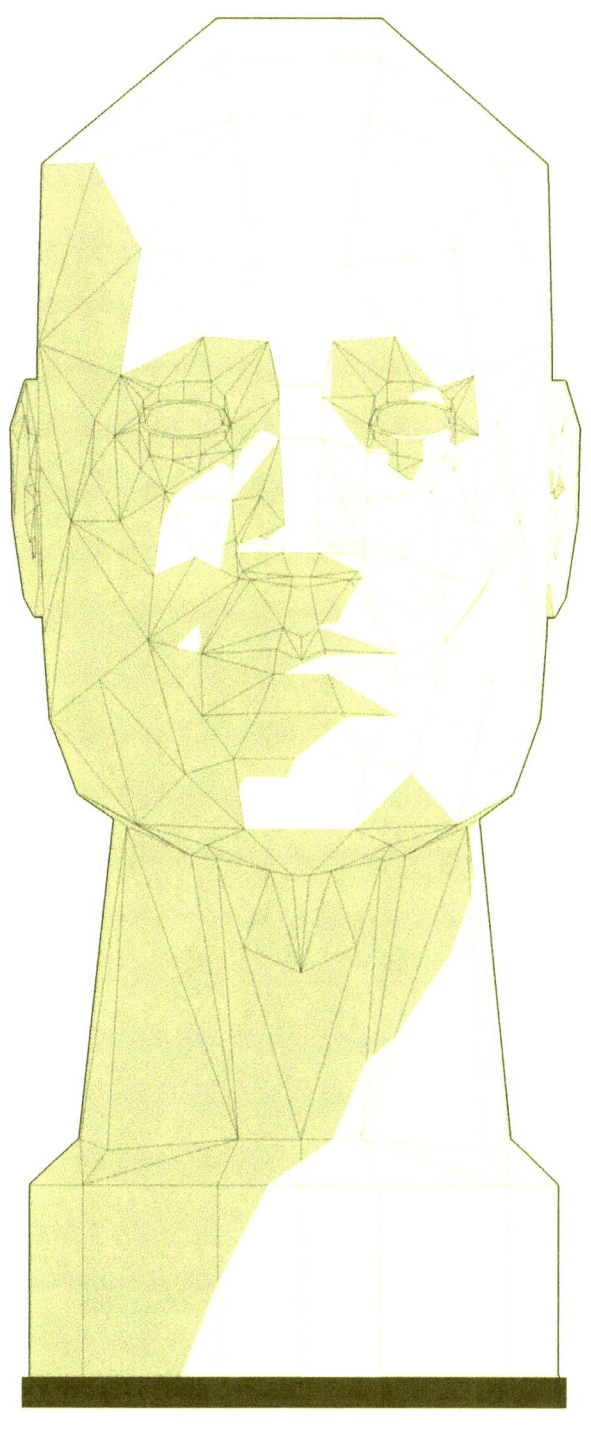

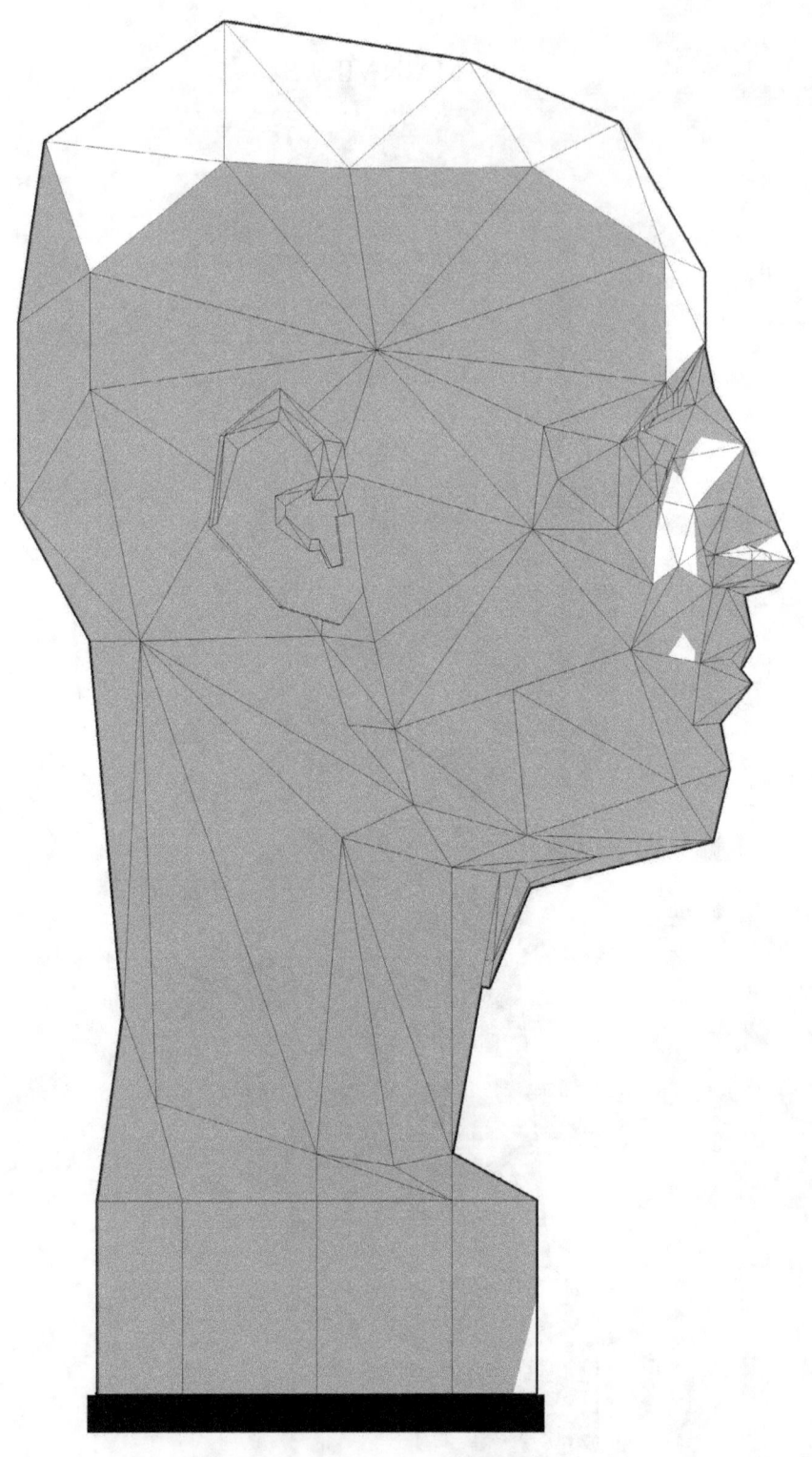

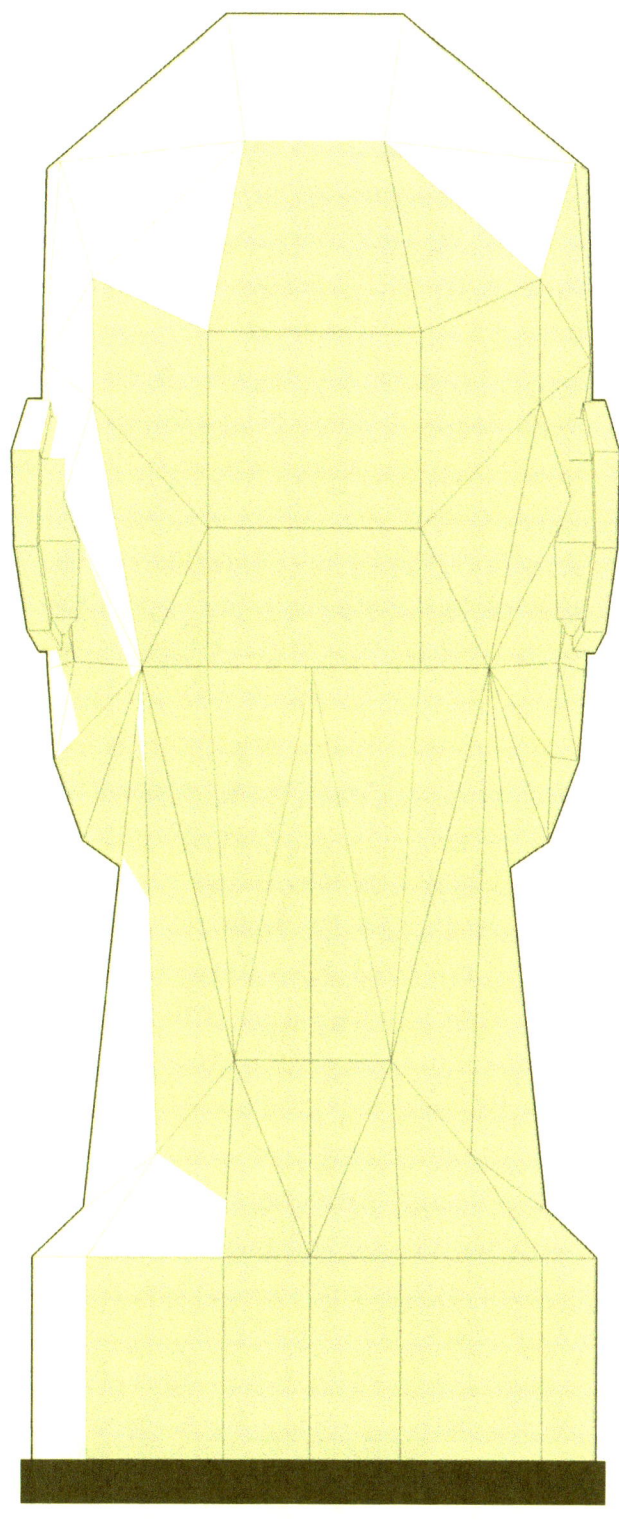

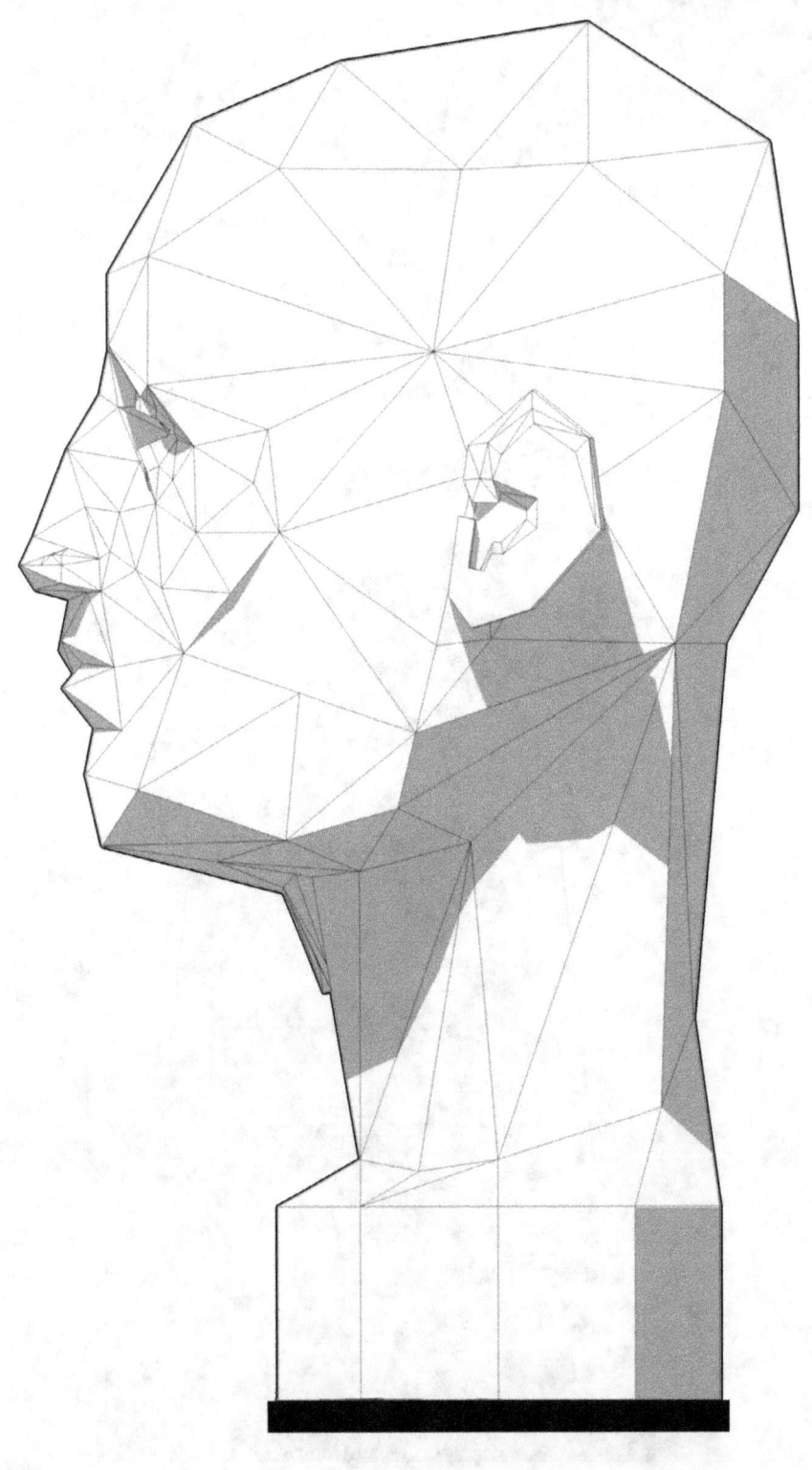

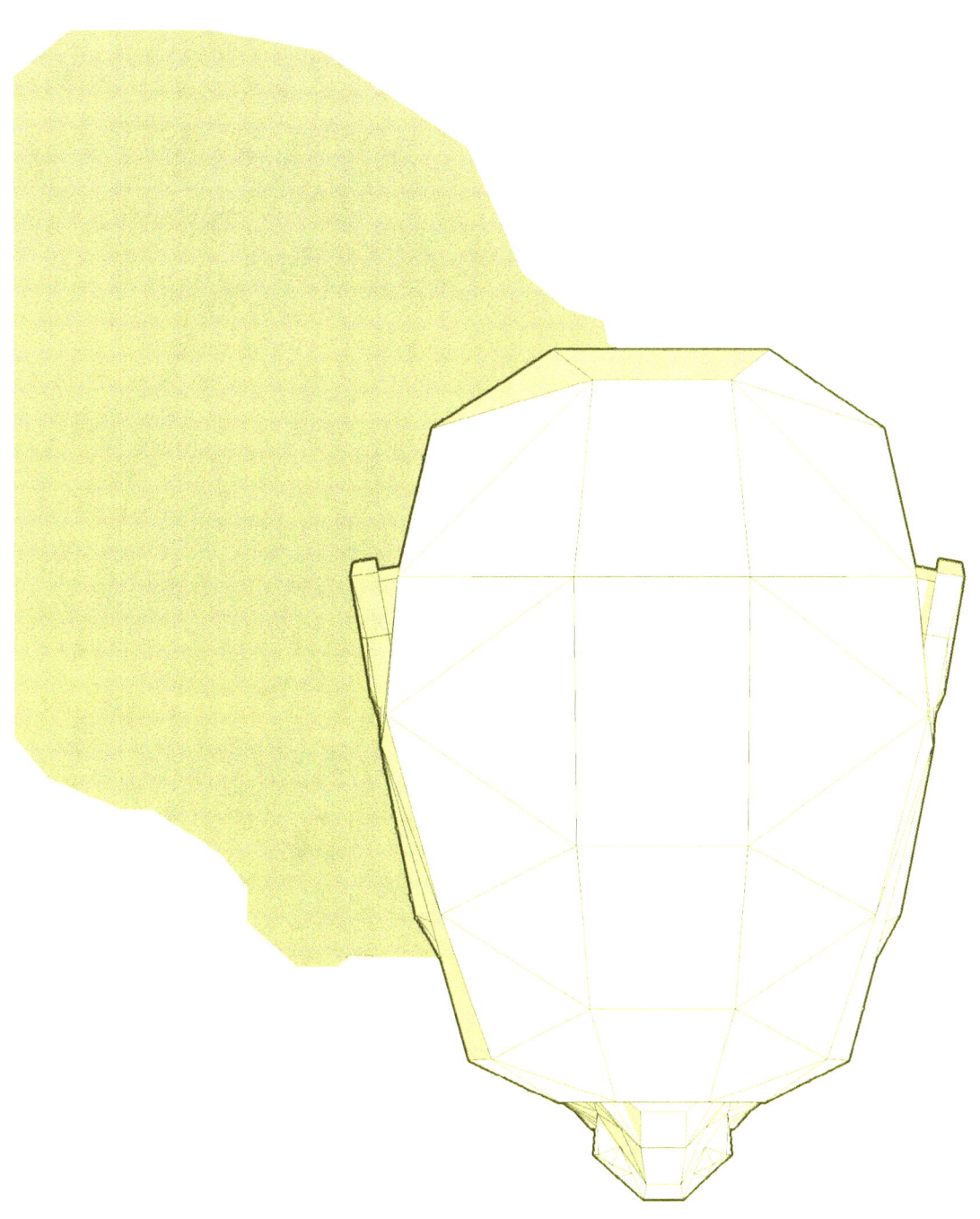

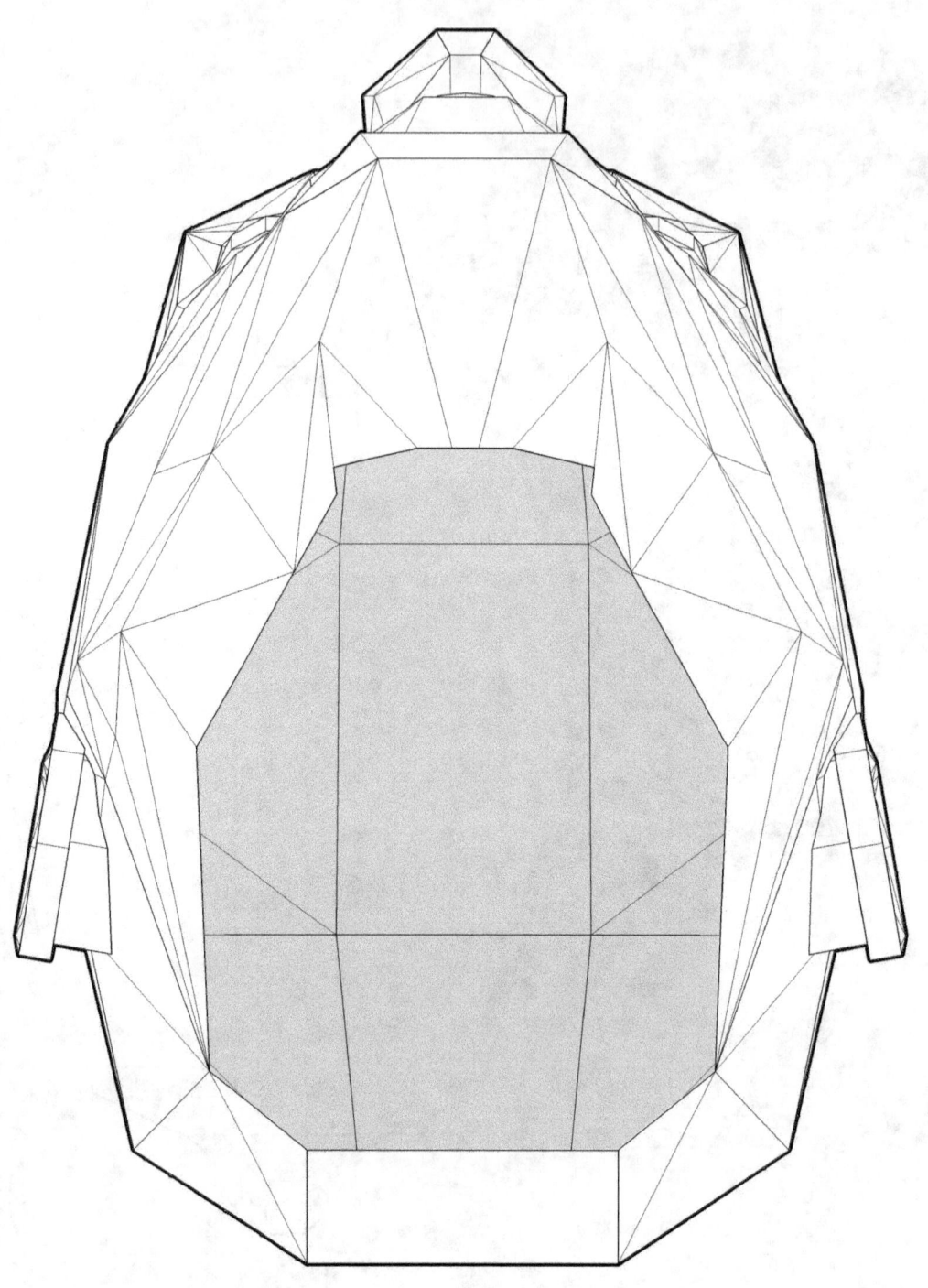

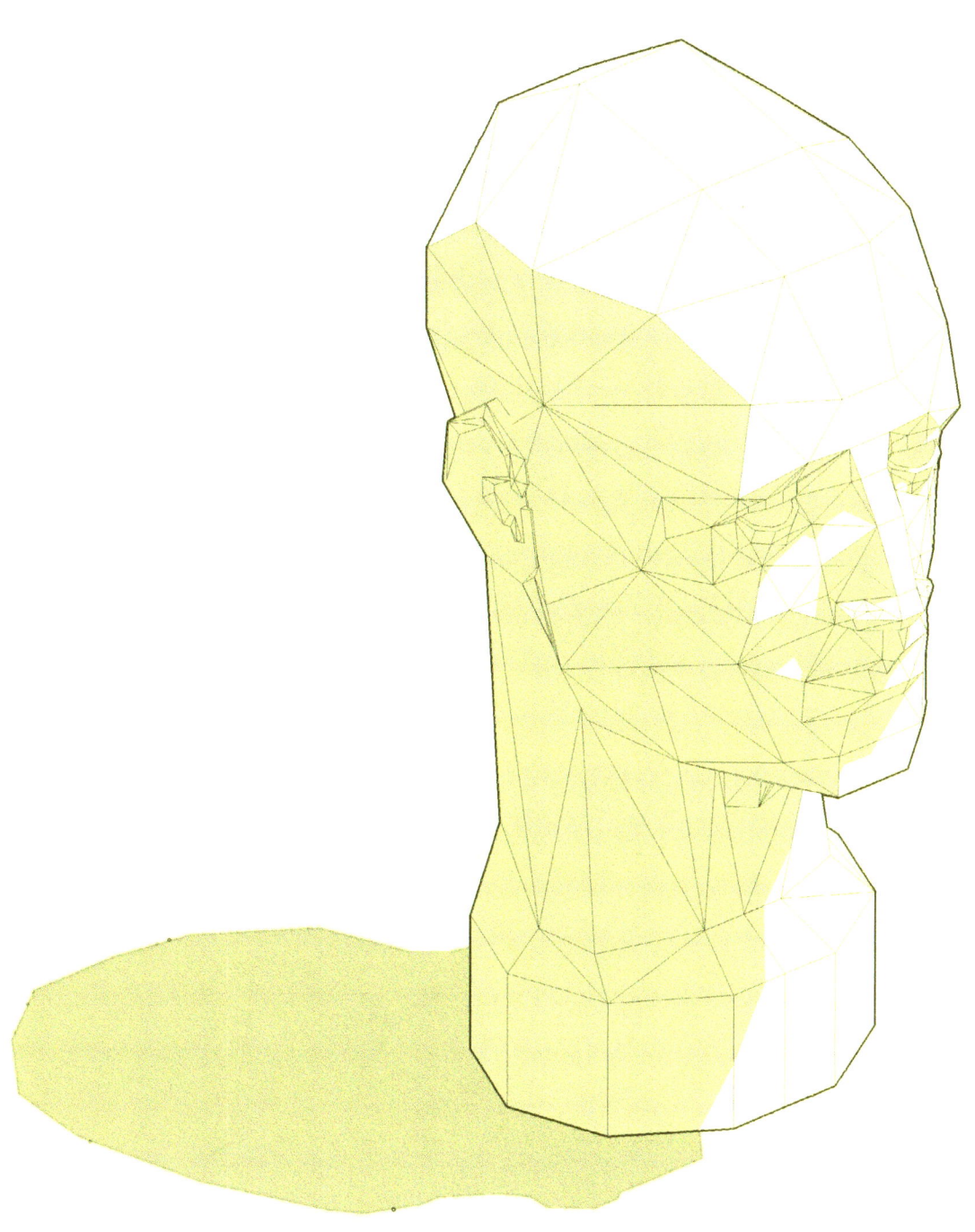

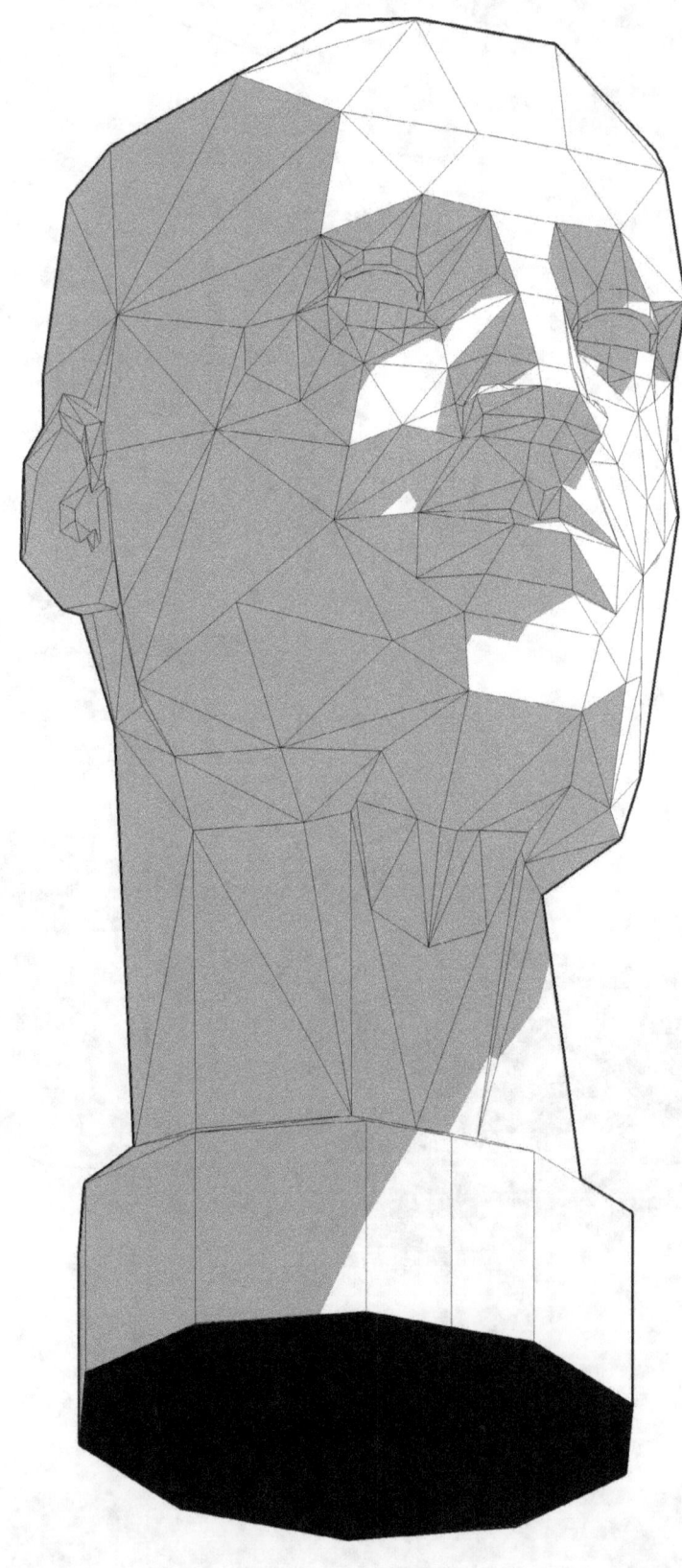

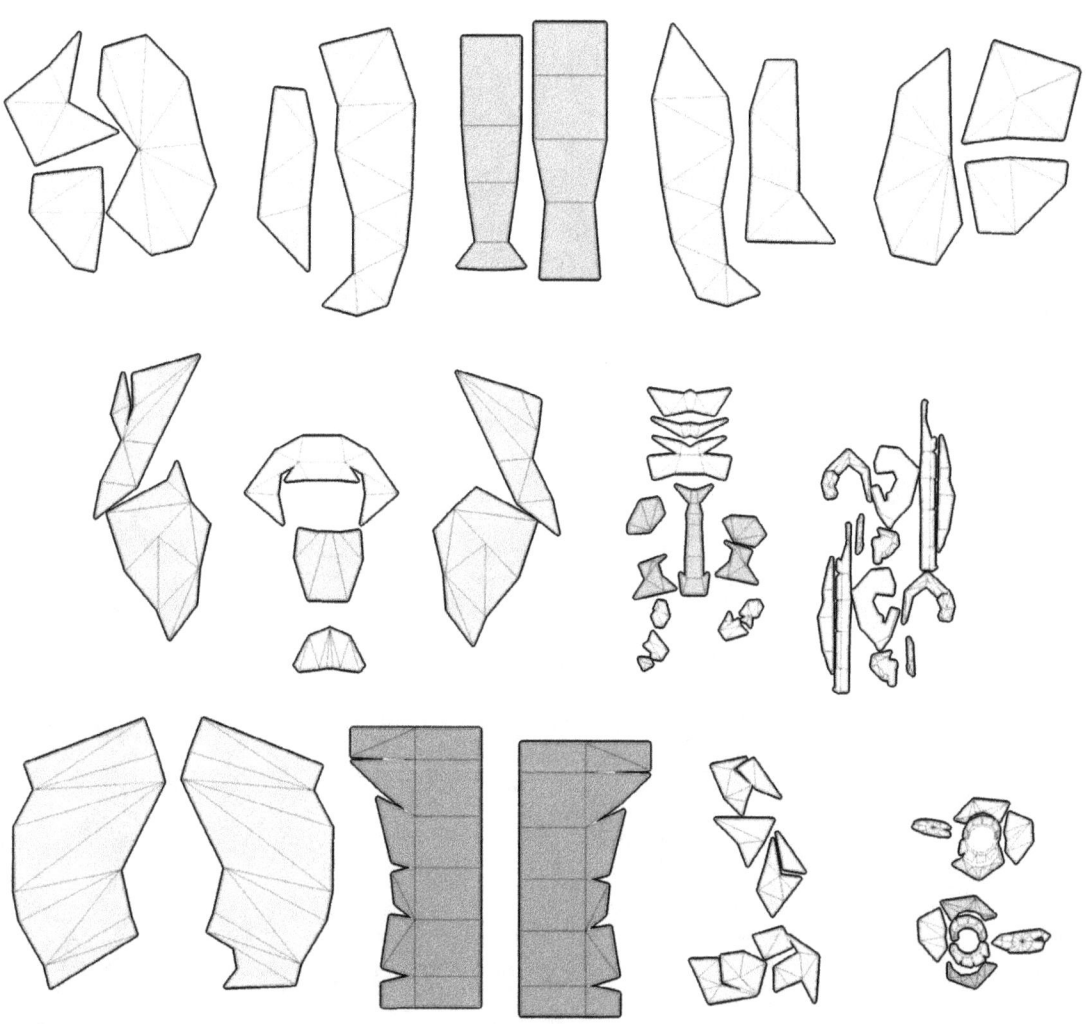

All the templates.

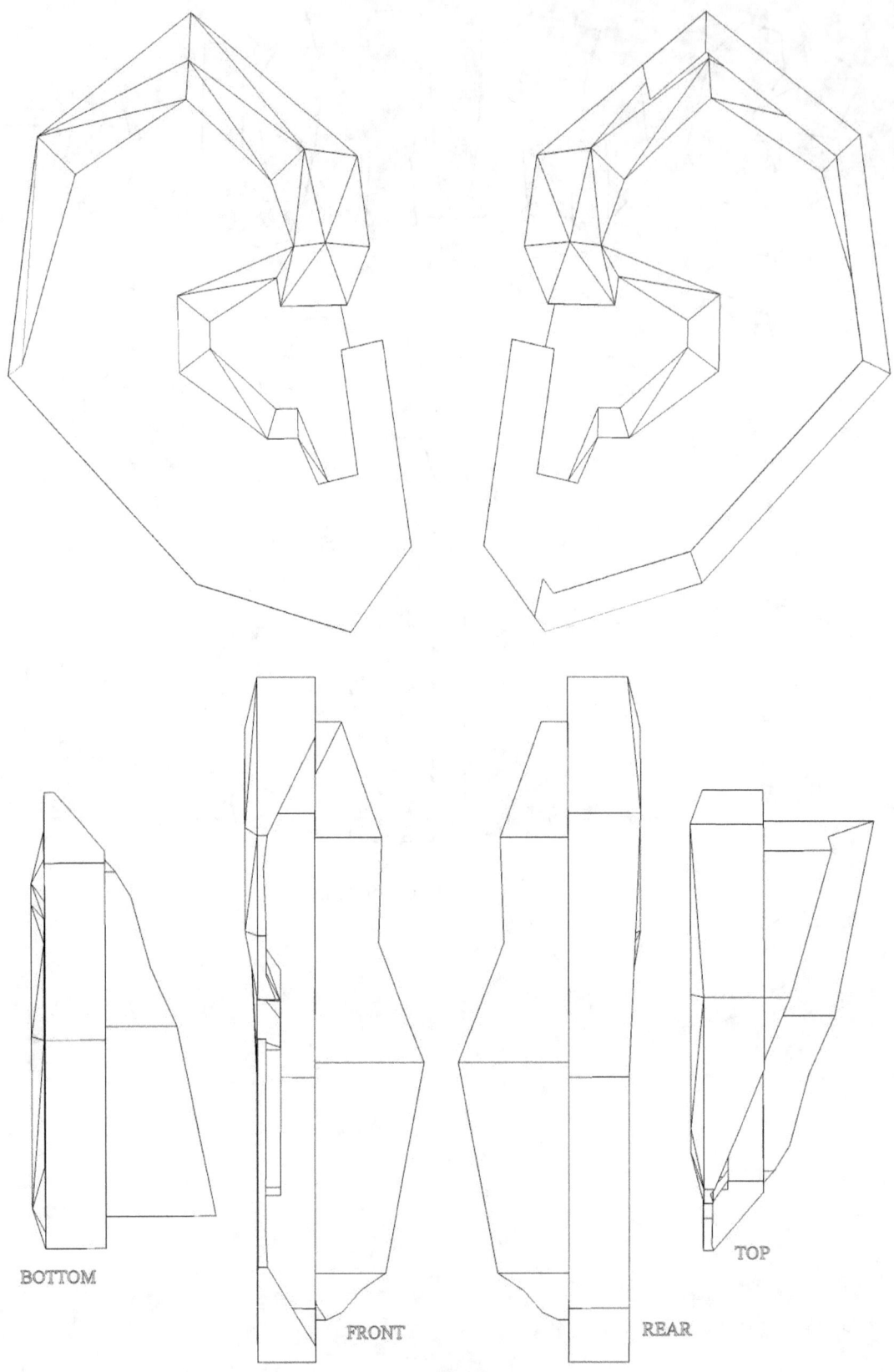

BOTTOM

FRONT

REAR

TOP

Close up of the ears.

PART 3

Templates

For the paperback version: scan the following pages and print them out on 8.5X11" cover stock. Cover stock is heavy weight paper available at any office supply store. Or, trace over the lines and transfer the drawings to cover stock or, even better, cardboard. Save the original pages as a reference for assembling the model. See below for printing from ebooks. The Planar Head is also available as a Kindle book.

When cutting out the shapes cut along the inner edge of the black outline to ensure proper fit.

Once the shapes are cut out you can fold and tape them together. For best results just score the fold lines with a knife taking care not to cut all the way through. Removable, Clear vinyl tape is best or white artist's tape. Any color tape if you plan to paint the head. Use minimum tape until you are sure all is well. Then tape all joined edges. Do the outside and the inside, too, for added strength where needed.

Refer to the views in Part 2 to help figure out how the pieces fit together as well as the plates in Part 3. One logical way to proceed is to assemble the base and neck. Then, assemble the cranium. Assemble the jaw next and then the face: eyes, nose, mouth area, cheeks. Fit the face to the cranium and then add the jaws. Finally, attach the head to the neck. Use one piece of cover stock cut to size and shape for the eyeballs. You can wad up a piece of thin paper the right size and glue it in place on each side of the nose for the nostrils. Or use the craft product called paperclay as I did.

Part 4 shows some stages of assembly. The model is usable simply taped together. Tips for making it stronger and more durable are also included.

How to Print from an Ebook

You can print out the templates at the correct size from Kindle or other ebook formats. For example, download and install on your computer the free Kindle for PC* and follow these steps for each Plate:

1) Open The Planar Head Workbook. 2) Select View > Full Screen. 3) Print Screen button.** 4) Open image editing program.*** 5) Paste as New Image. 6) Crop image exactly on the top and bottom borders. 7) Resize image to 9.25" high for the first head at 300 ppi and 9.5" for the second. 8) Print.

* If you have a Kindle Alt+Shift+G will capture the current screen and save it as a jpg file in the documents folder. Save to a USB drive and transfer to your computer.

** Print Screen will capture an image of your entire screen on the Clipboard at screen resolution. The job is a little easier if you use a special screen capture program like PrintKey.

*** I use PaintShop. The open source, free, program called Gimp will work.

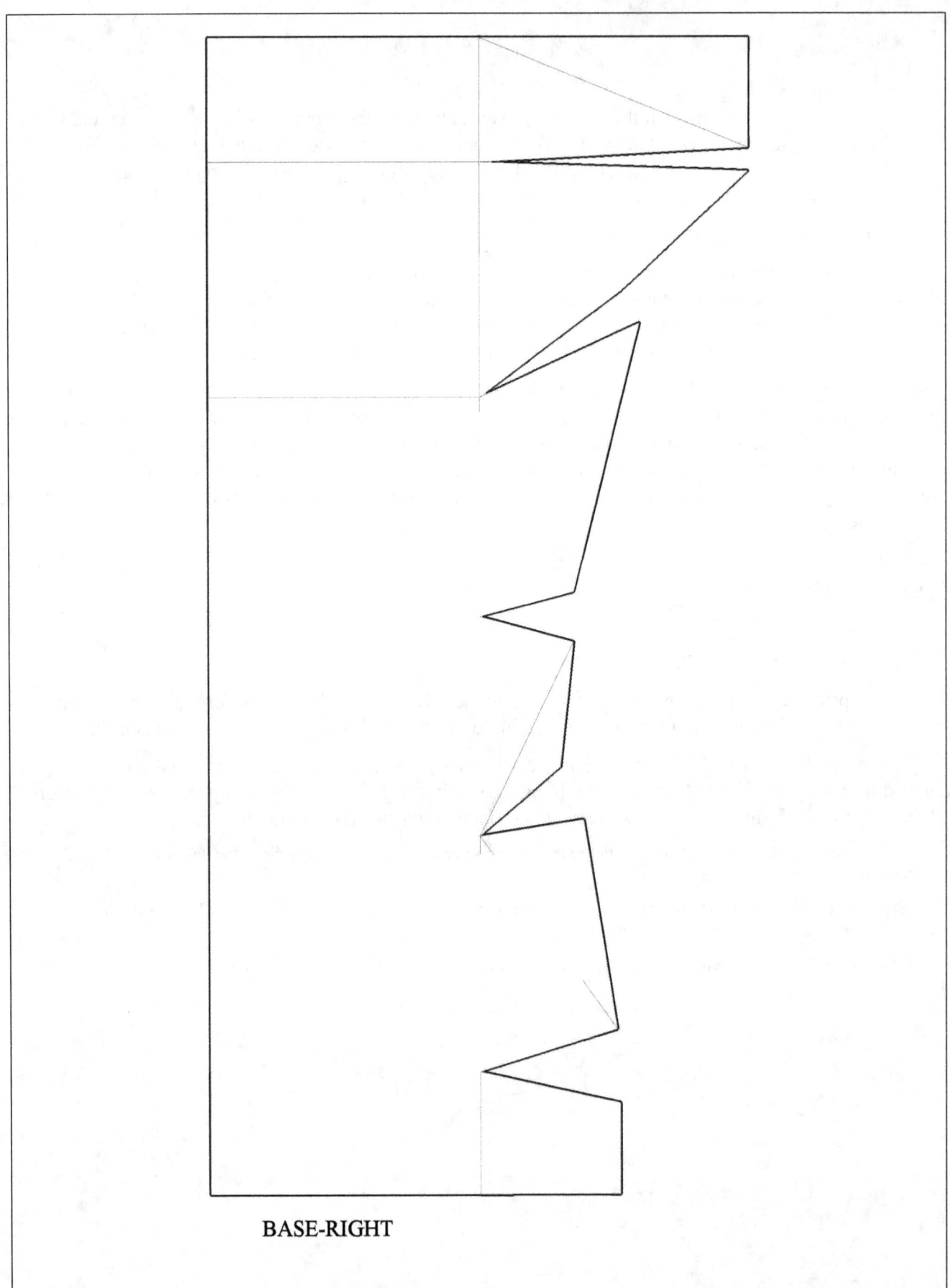

BASE-RIGHT

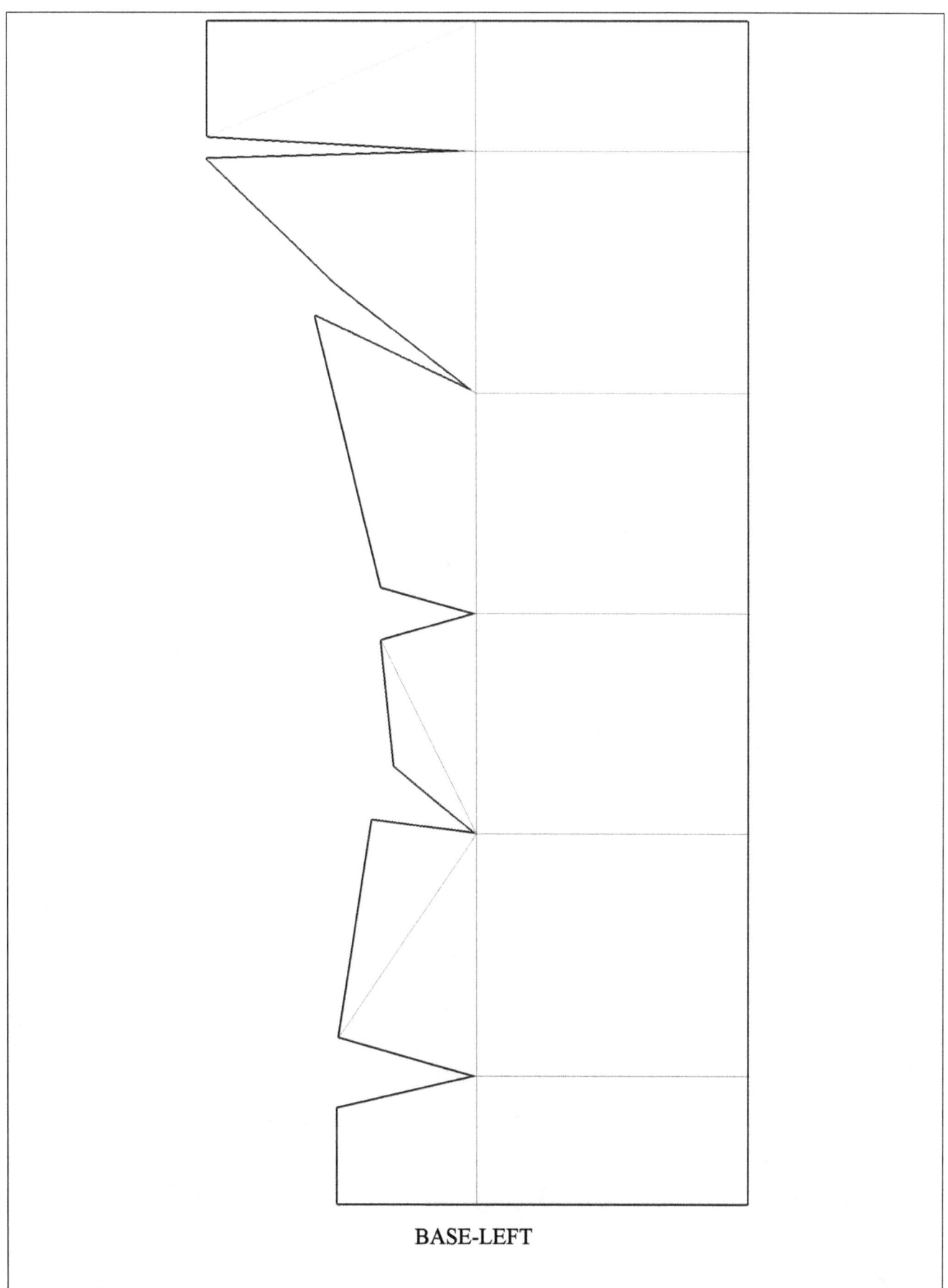

BASE-LEFT

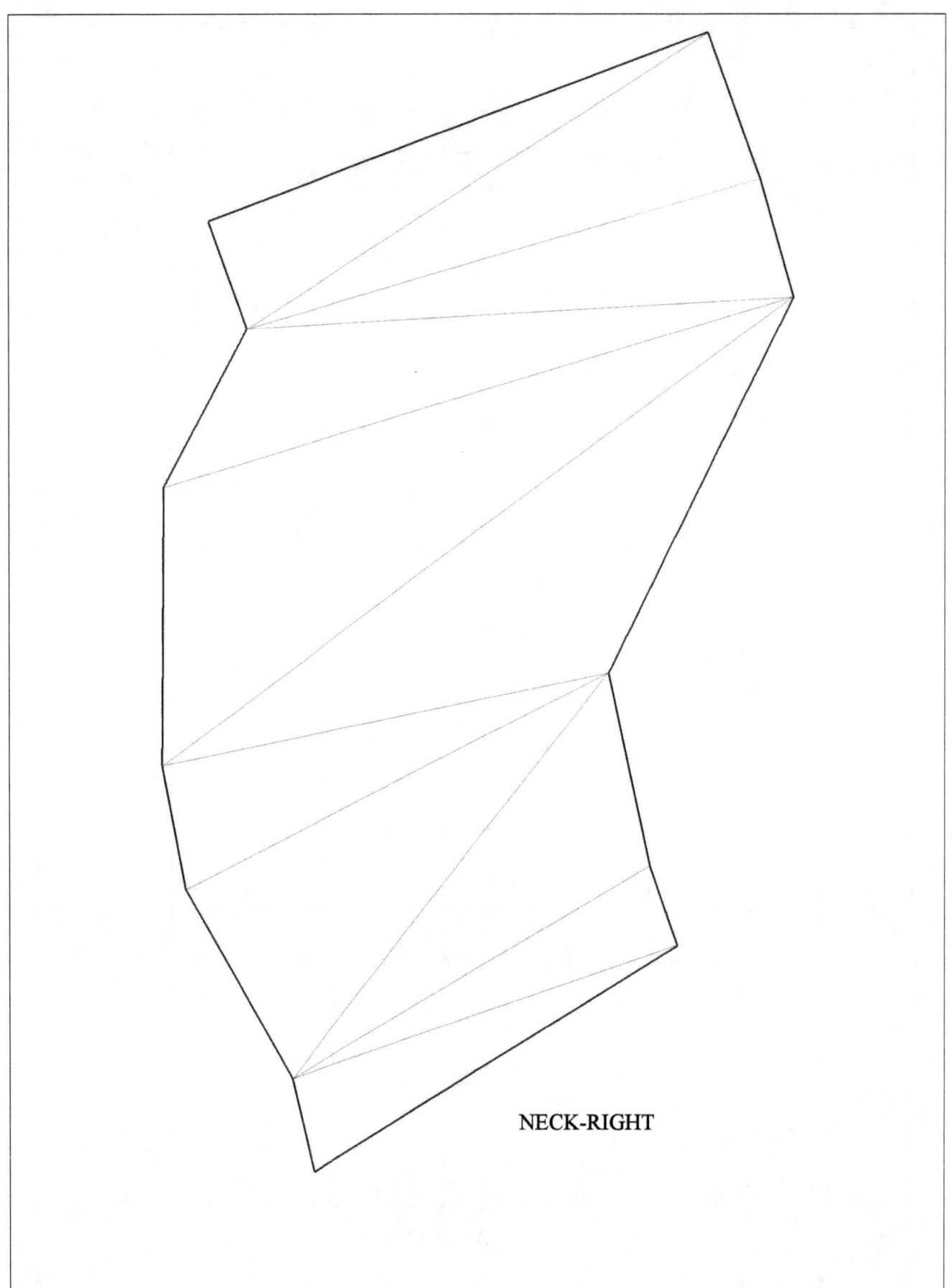

NECK-RIGHT

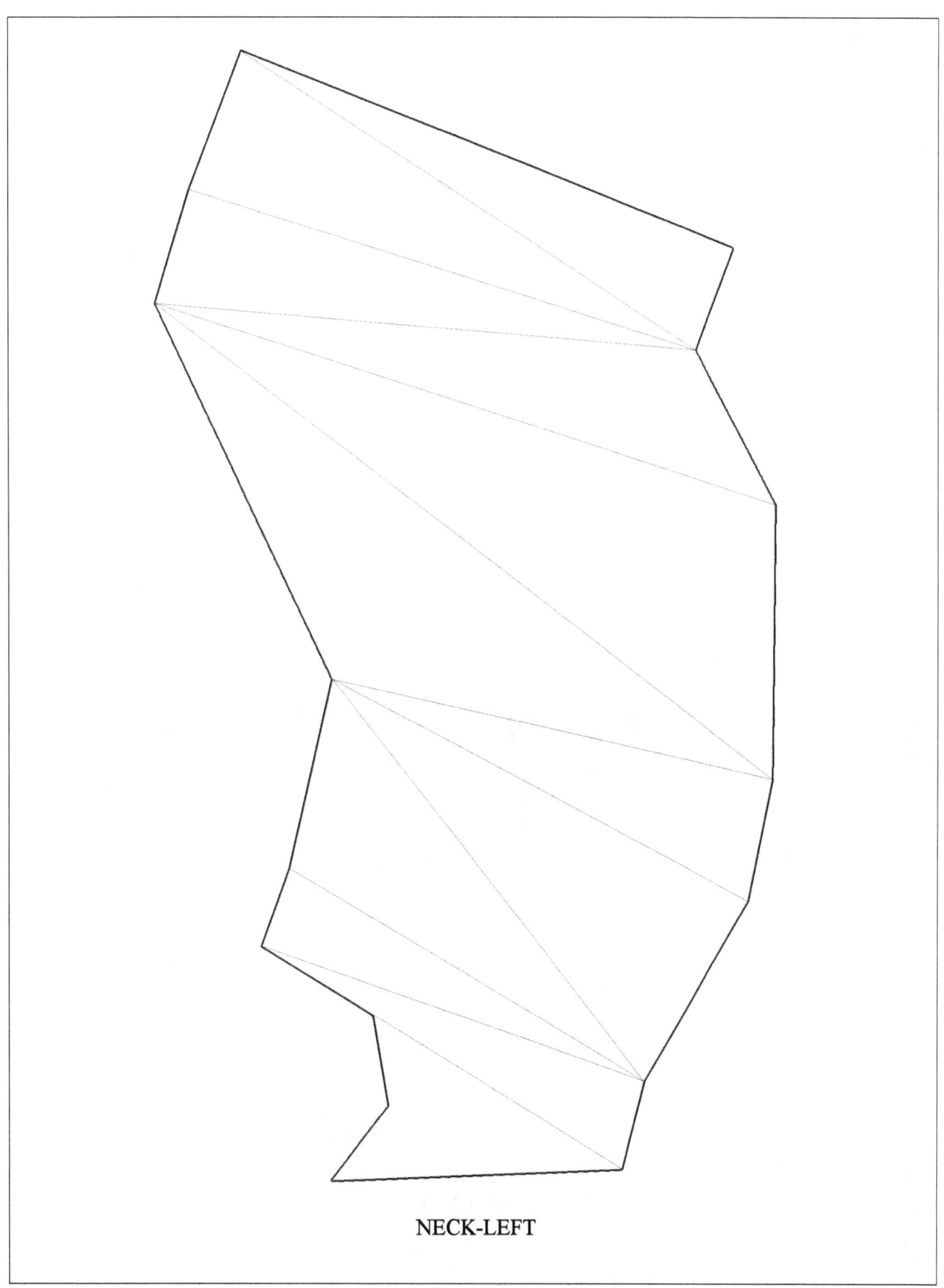

NECK-LEFT

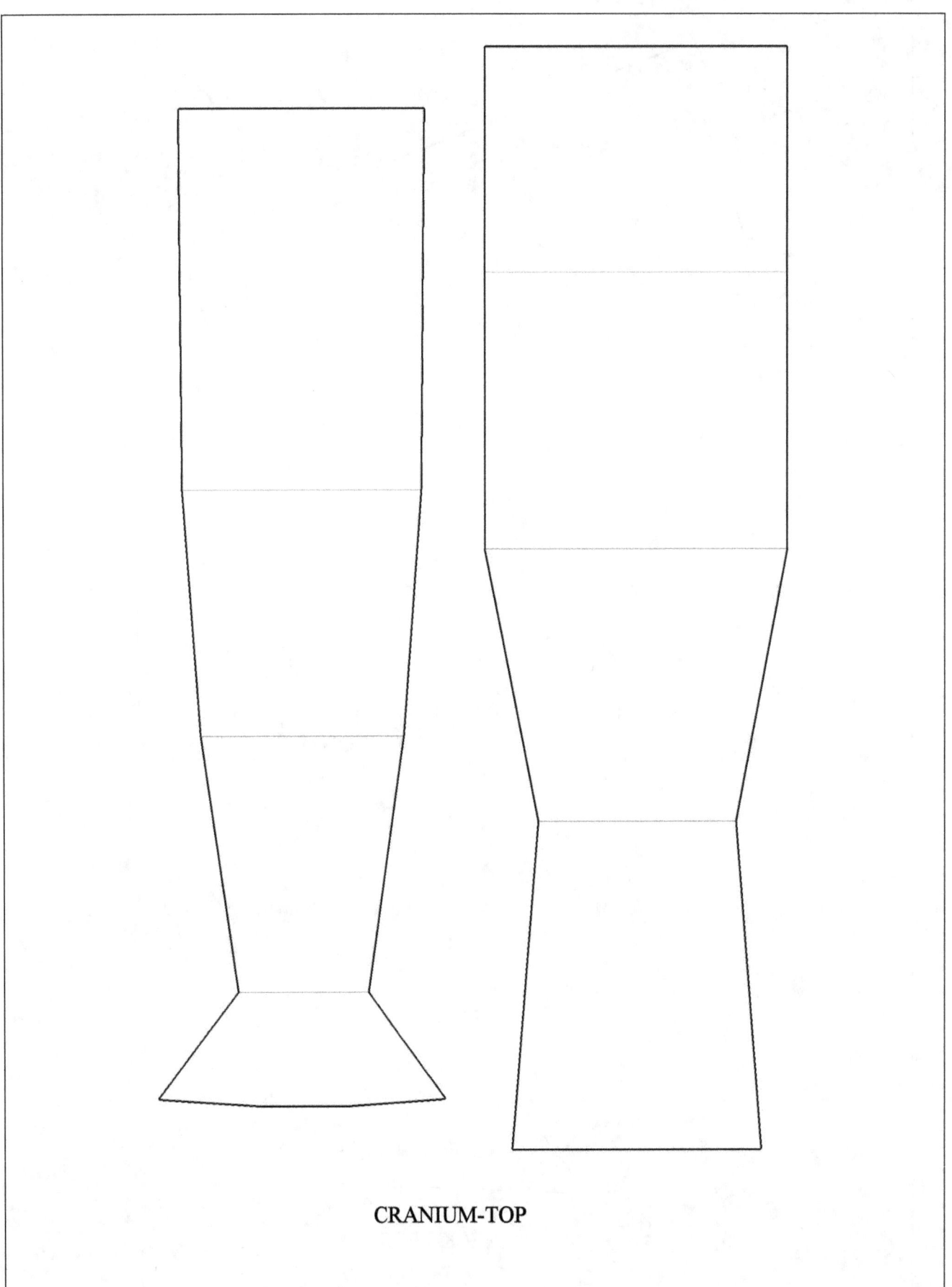

CRANIUM-TOP

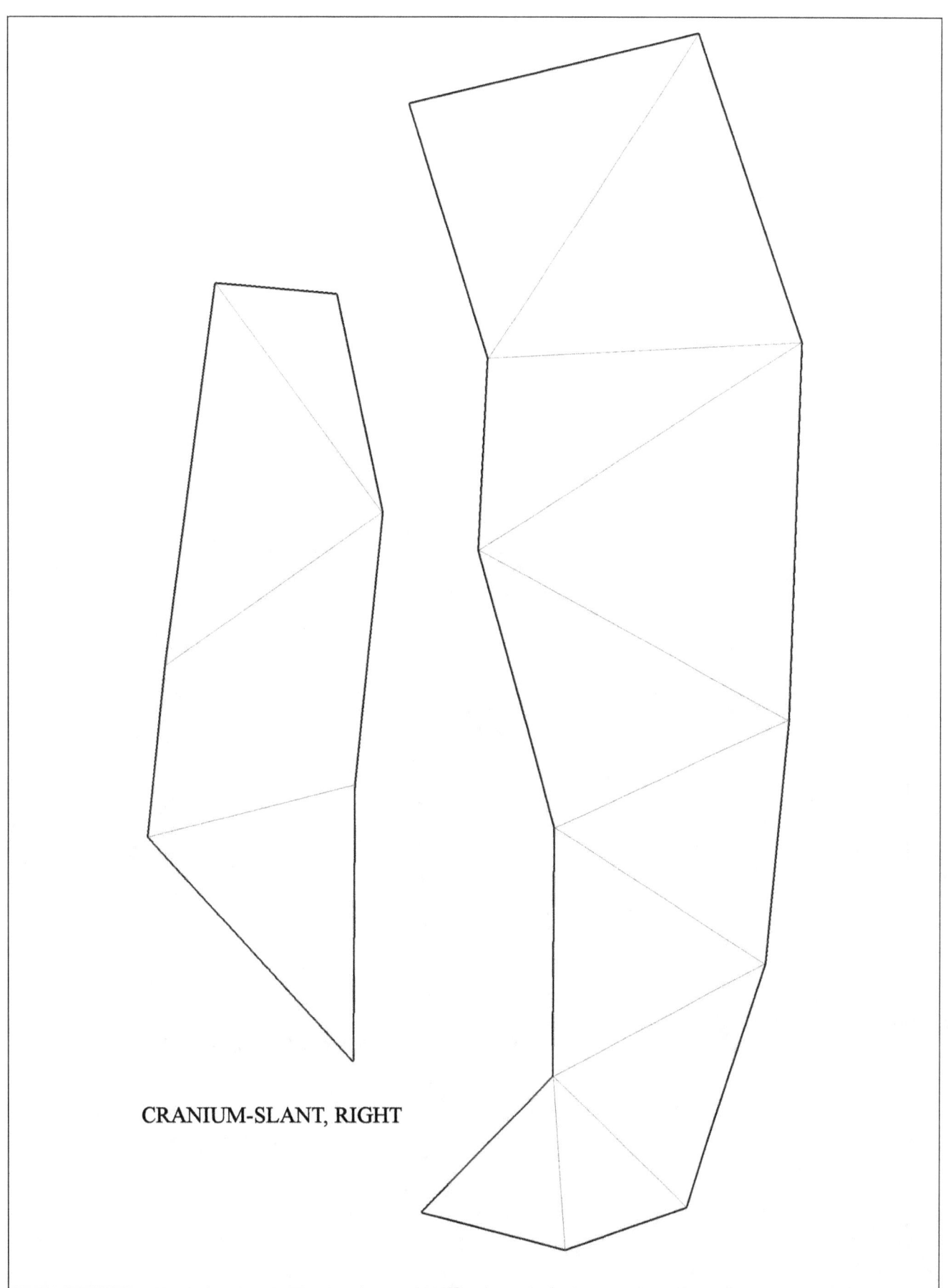

CRANIUM-SLANT, RIGHT

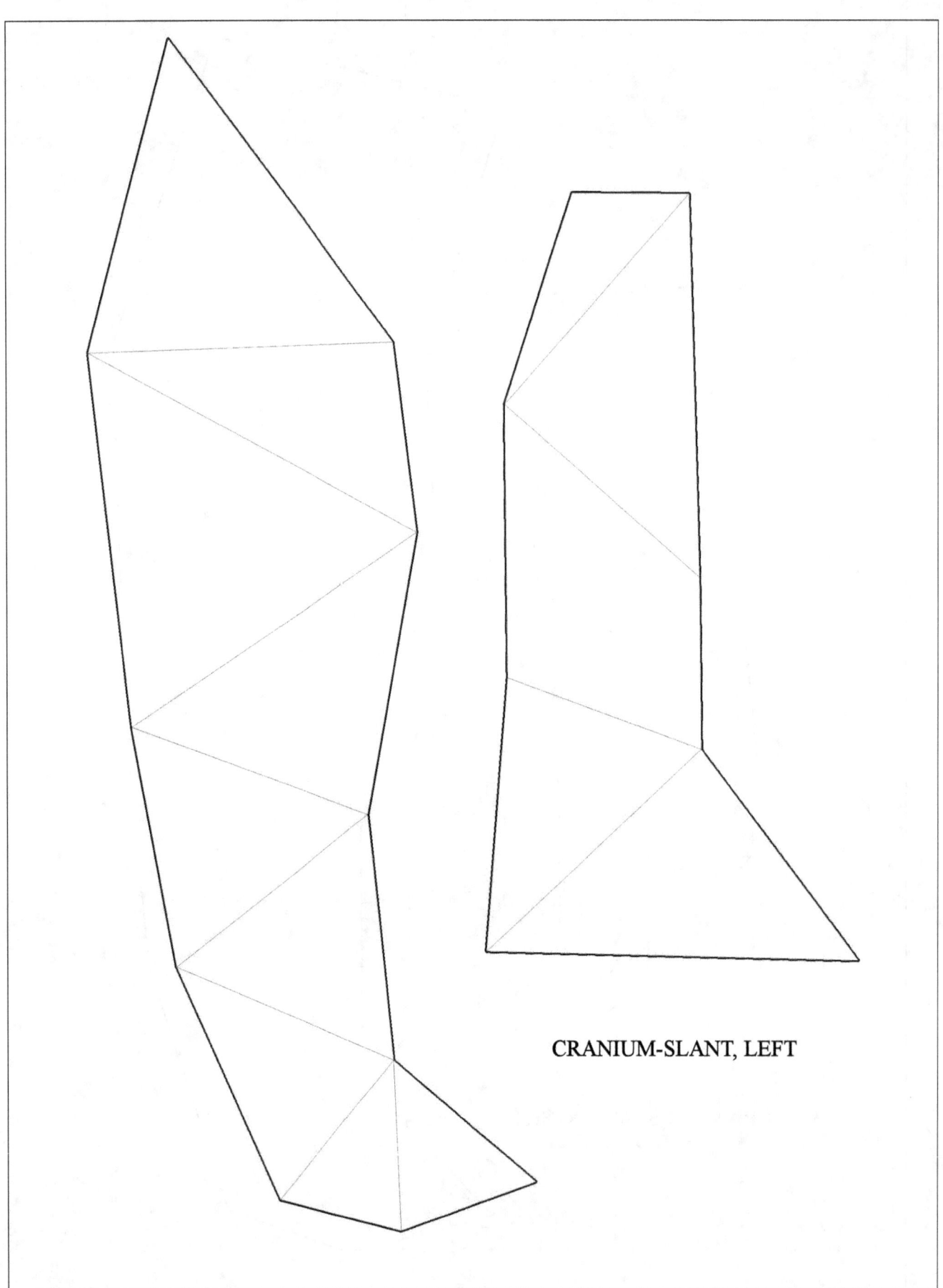

CRANIUM-SLANT, LEFT

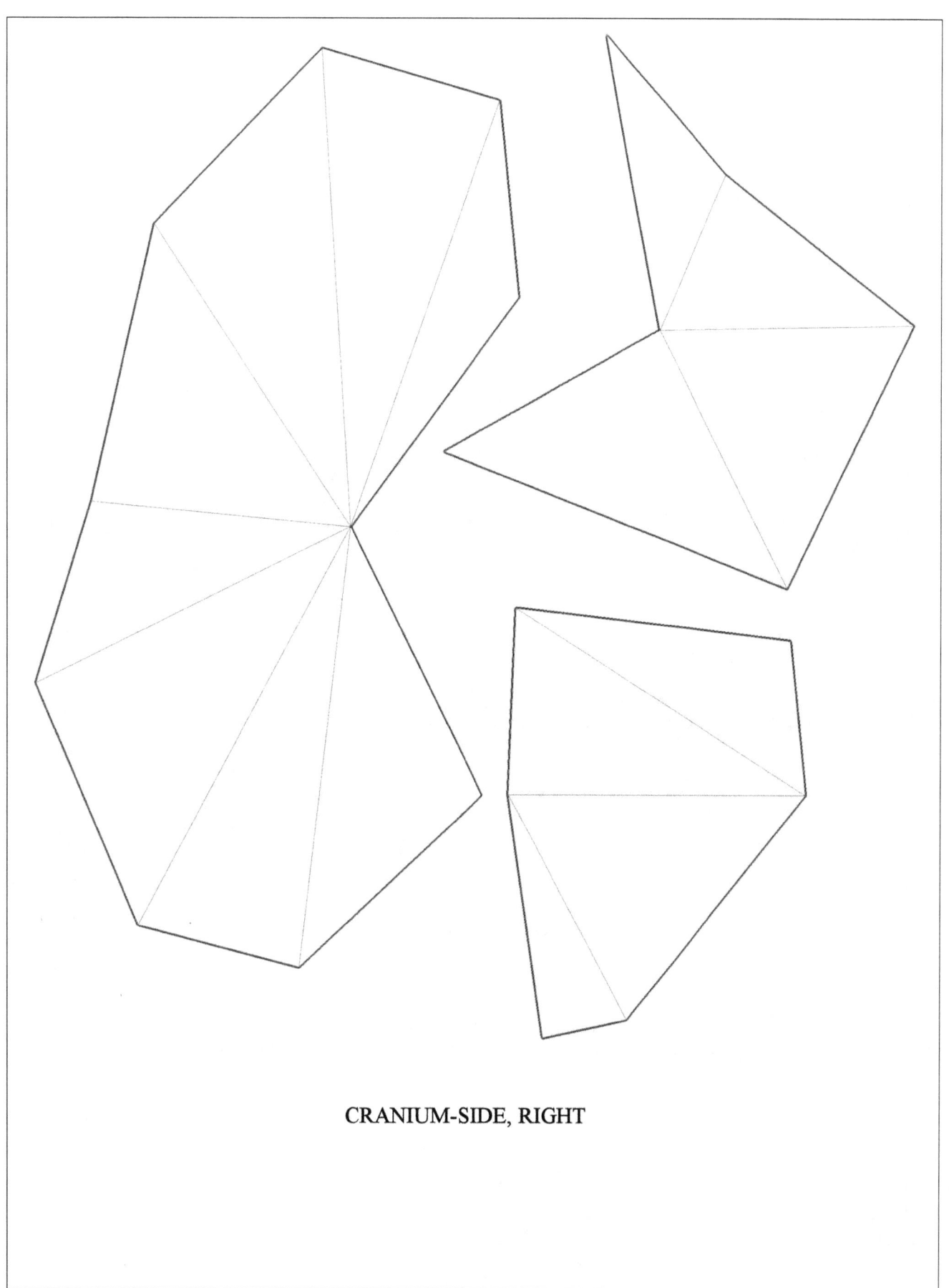

CRANIUM-SIDE, RIGHT

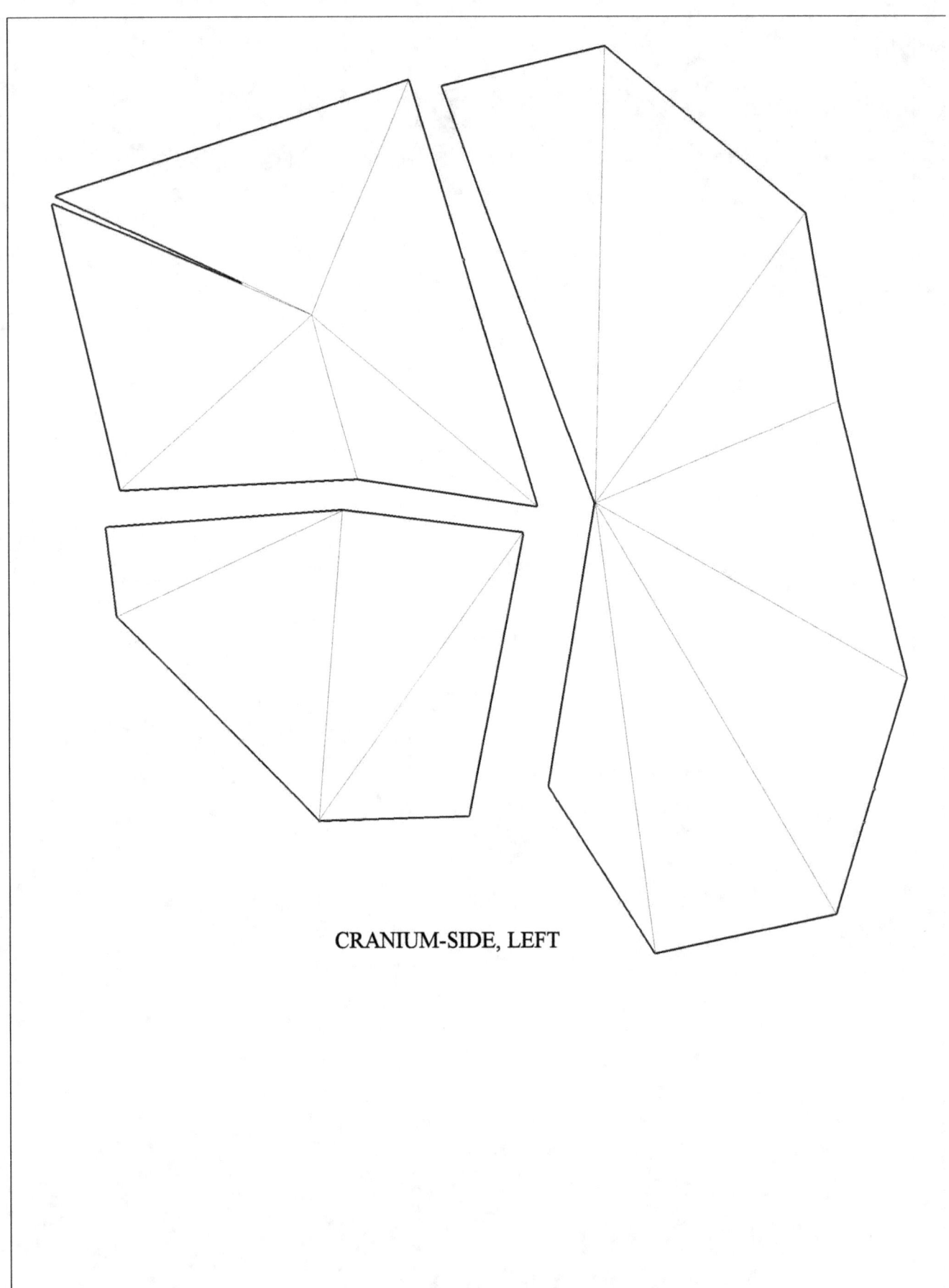

CRANIUM-SIDE, LEFT

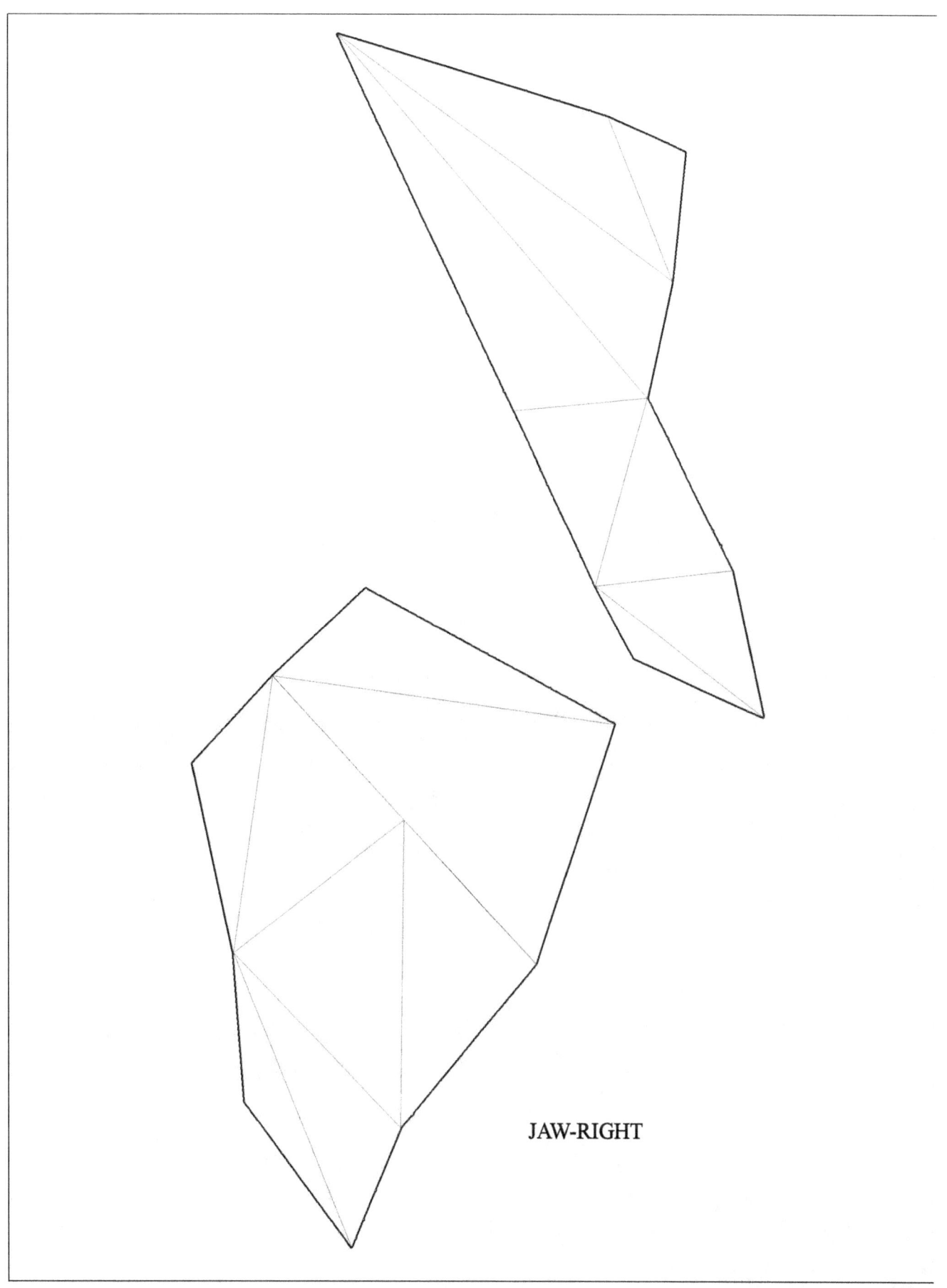

JAW-RIGHT

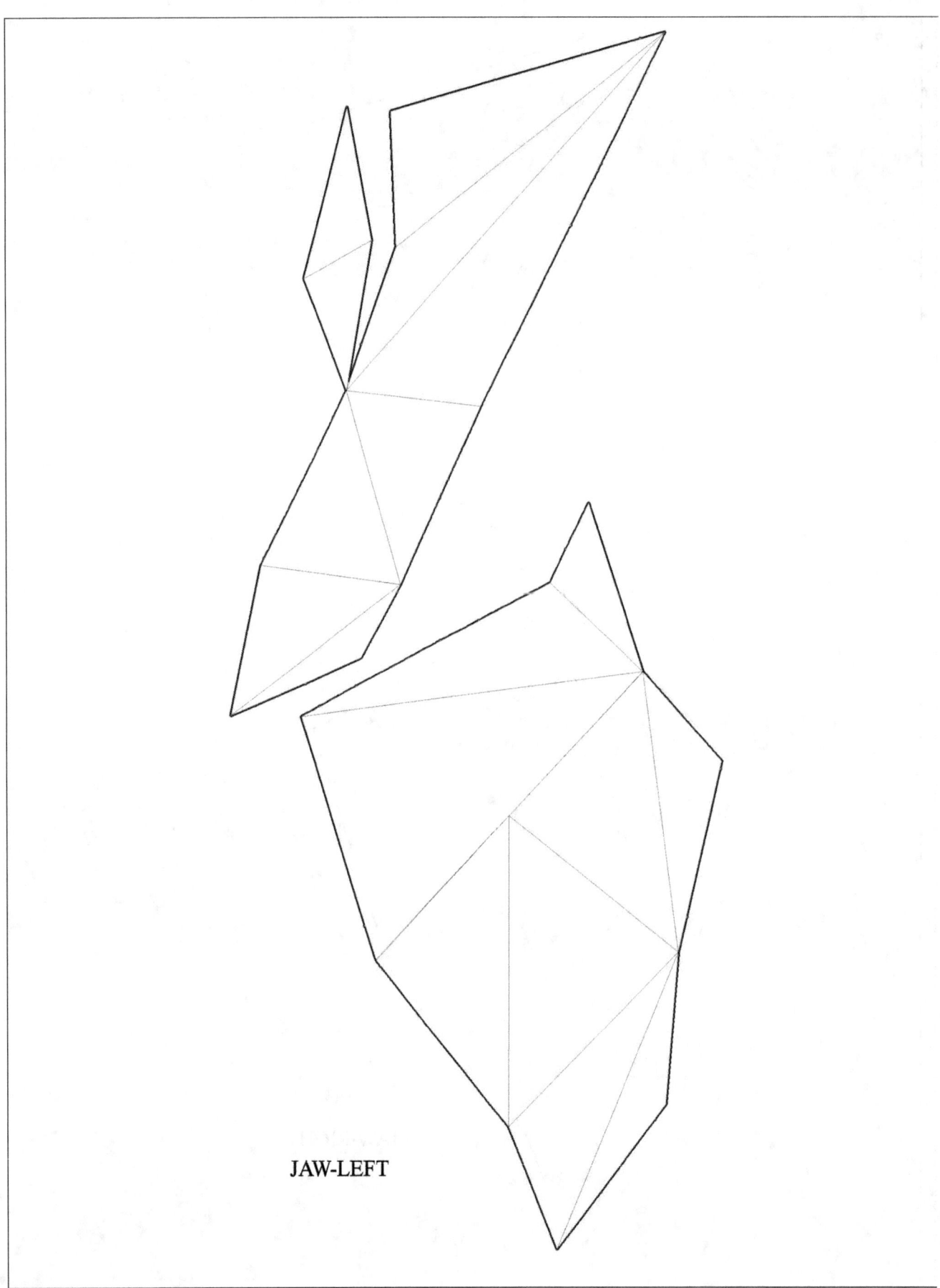

JAW-LEFT

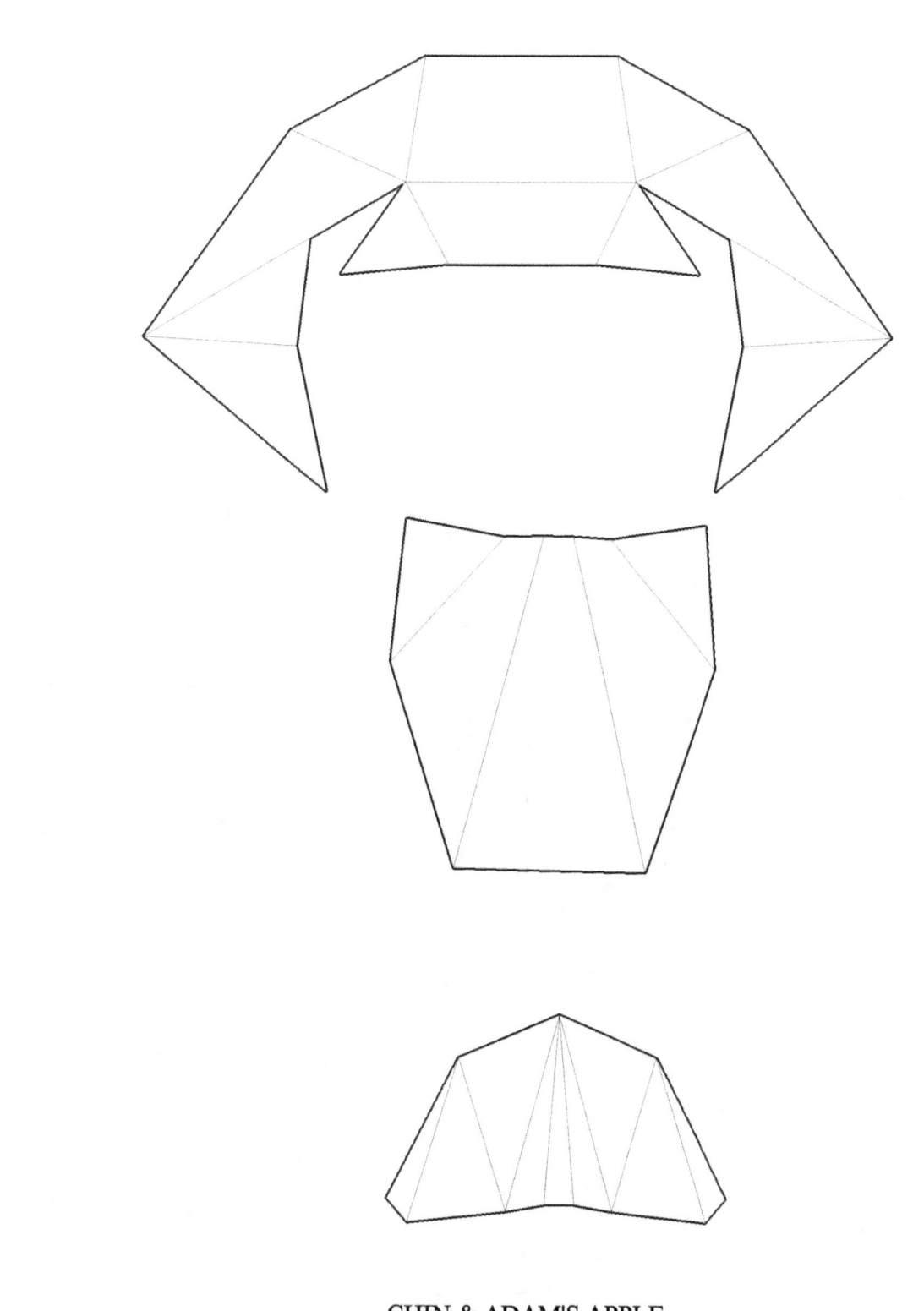

CHIN & ADAM'S APPLE

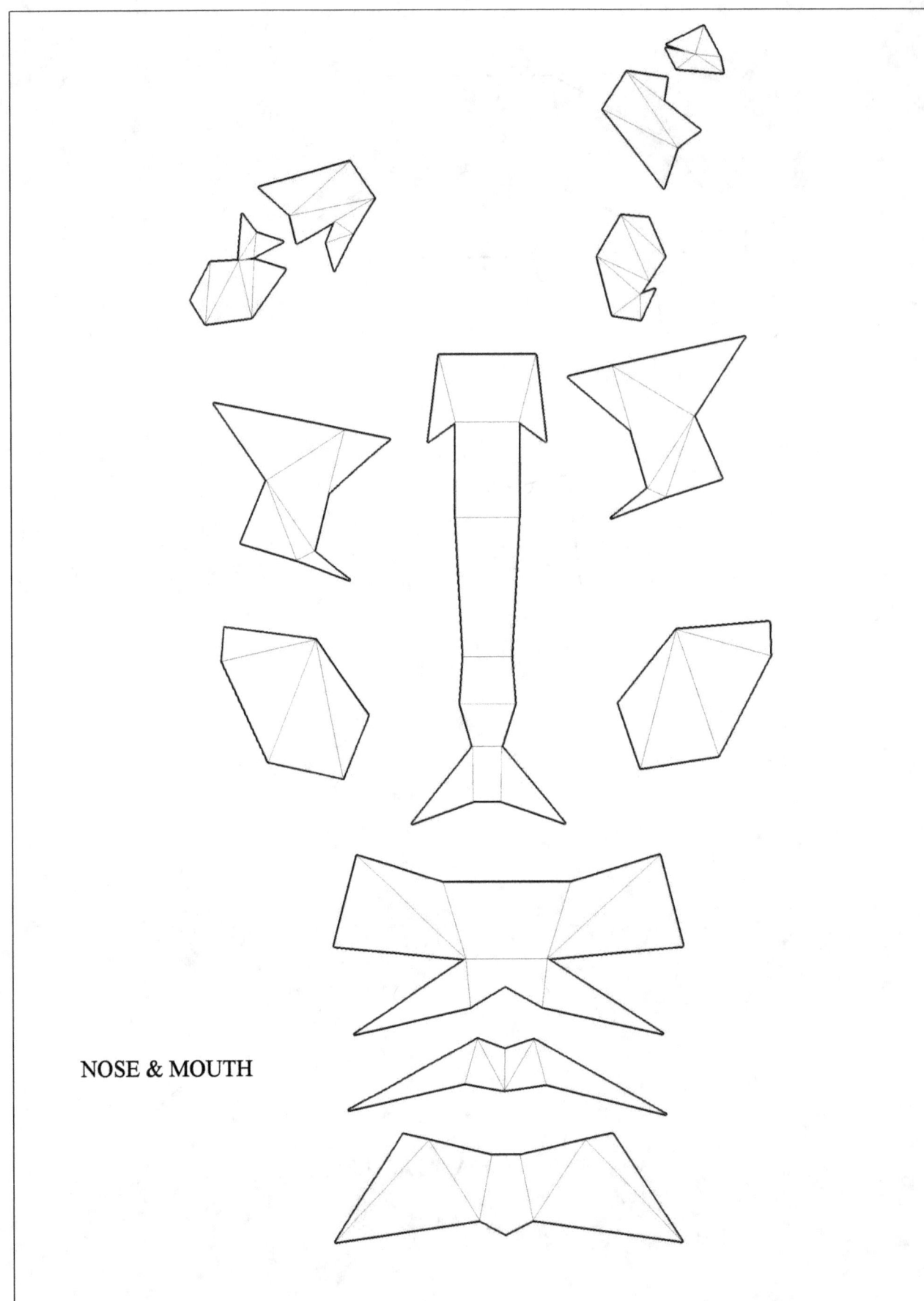

NOSE & MOUTH

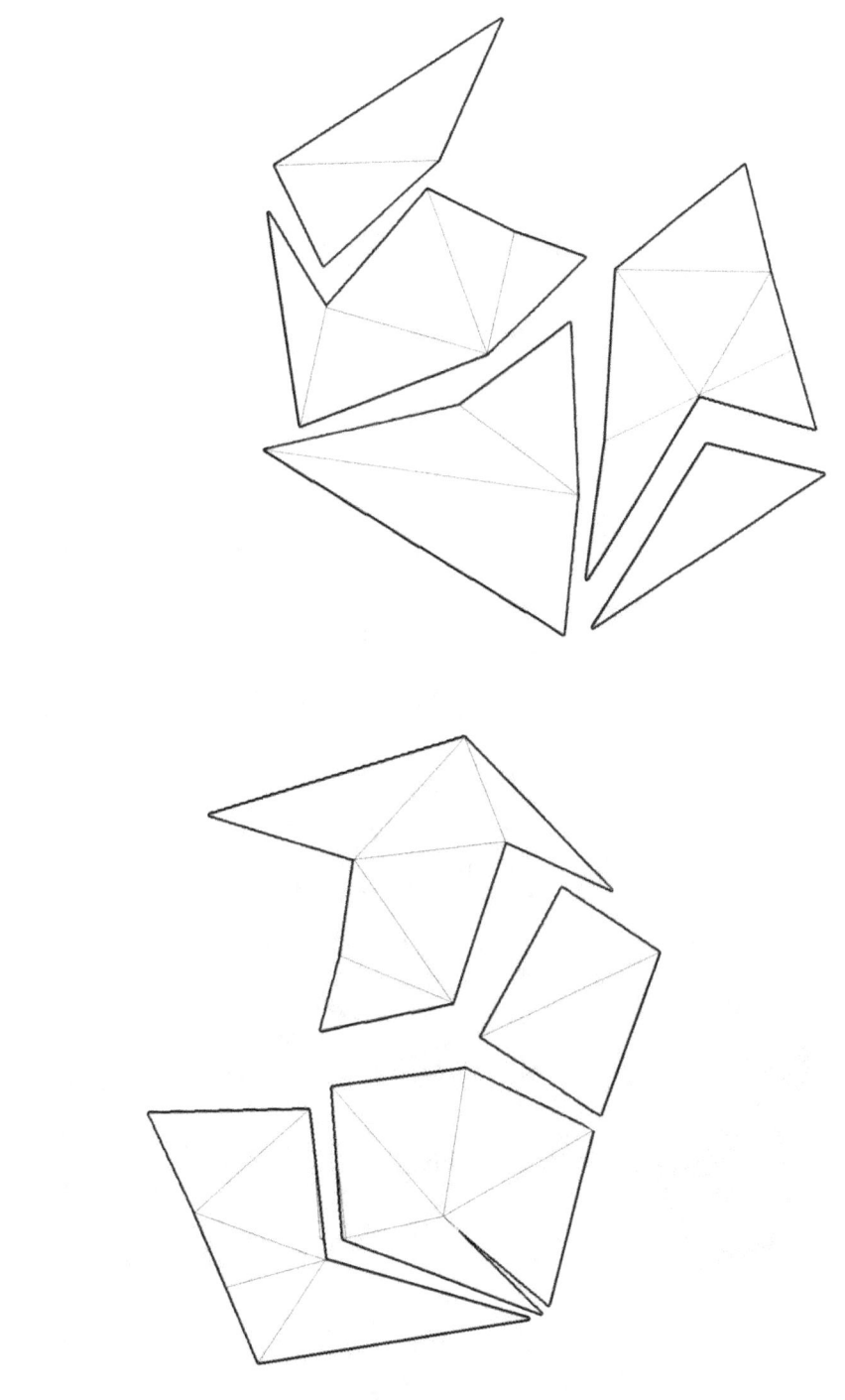

UNDER EYES RIGHT & LEFT

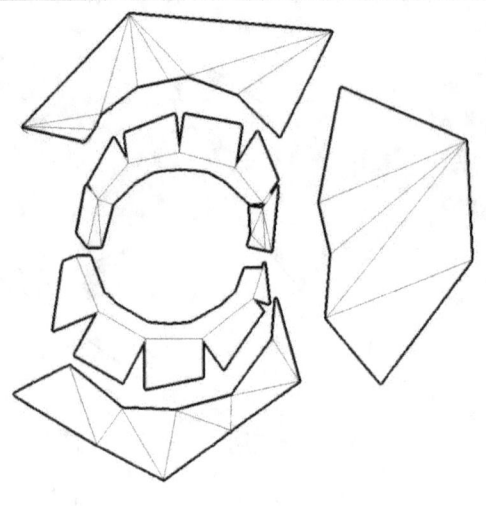

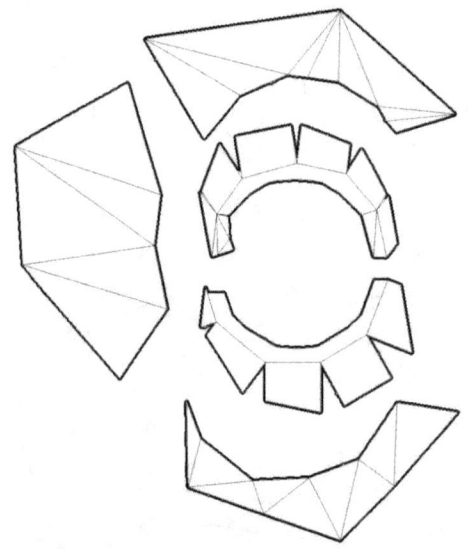

EYES

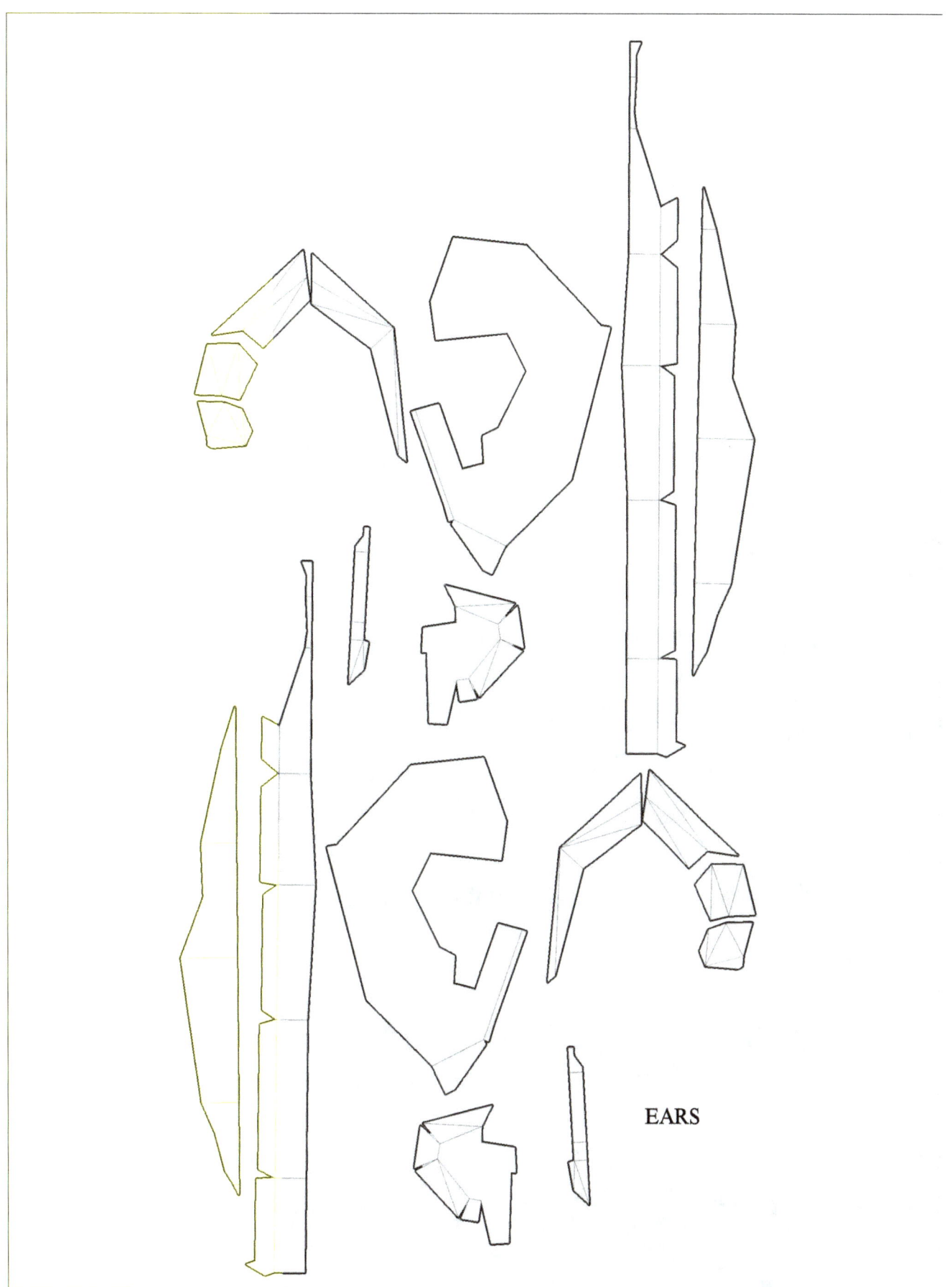

EARS

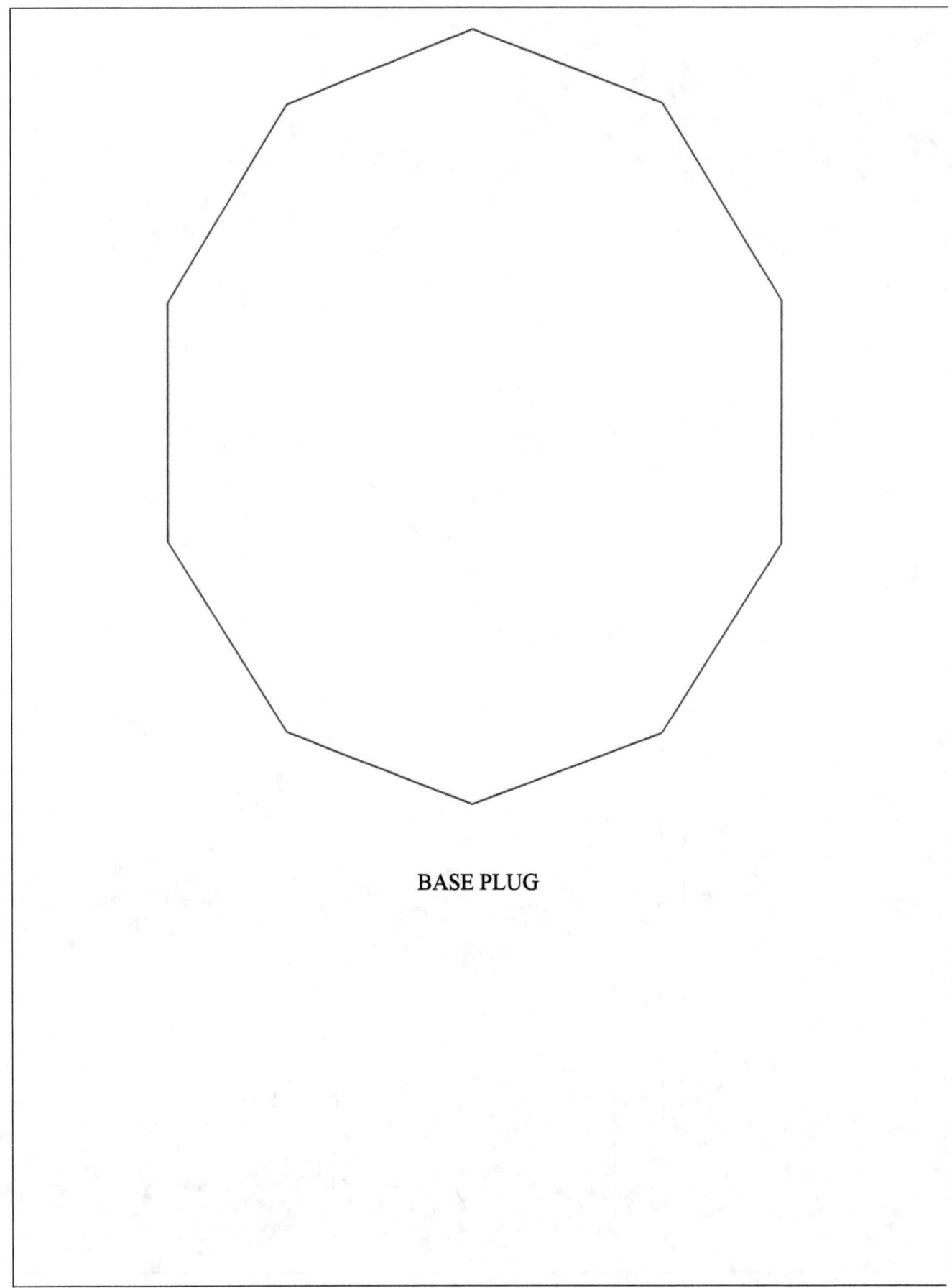

BASE PLUG

PART 4

Assembly Photos

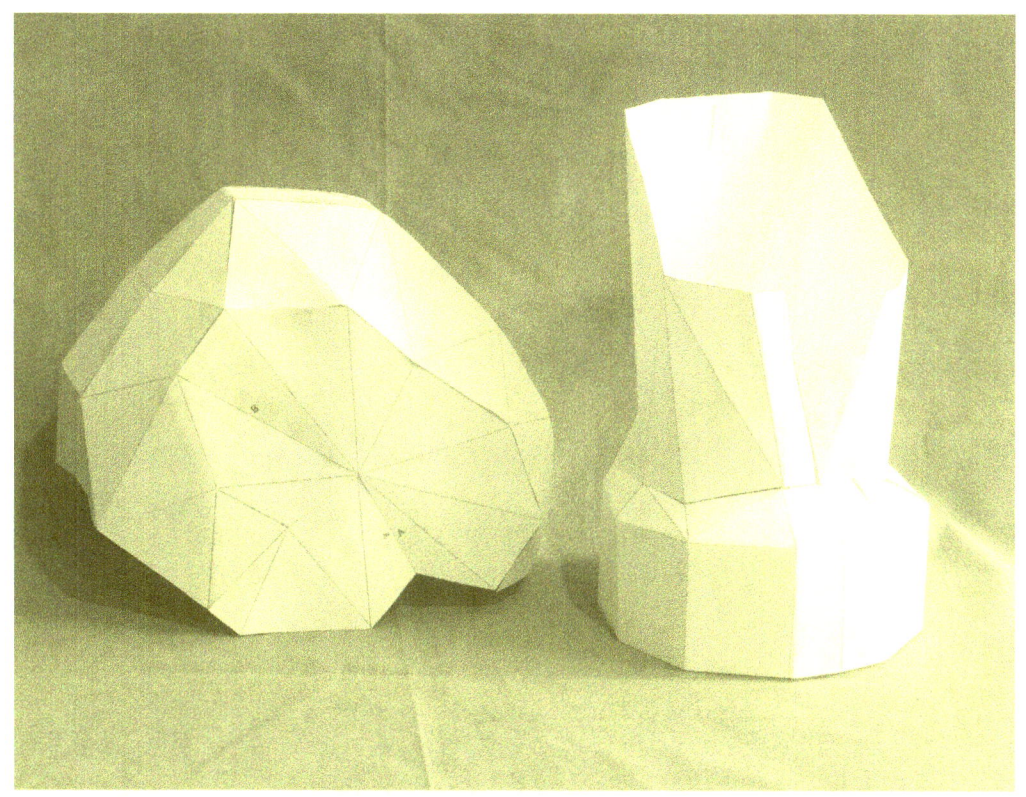

Cranium - Neck & Base

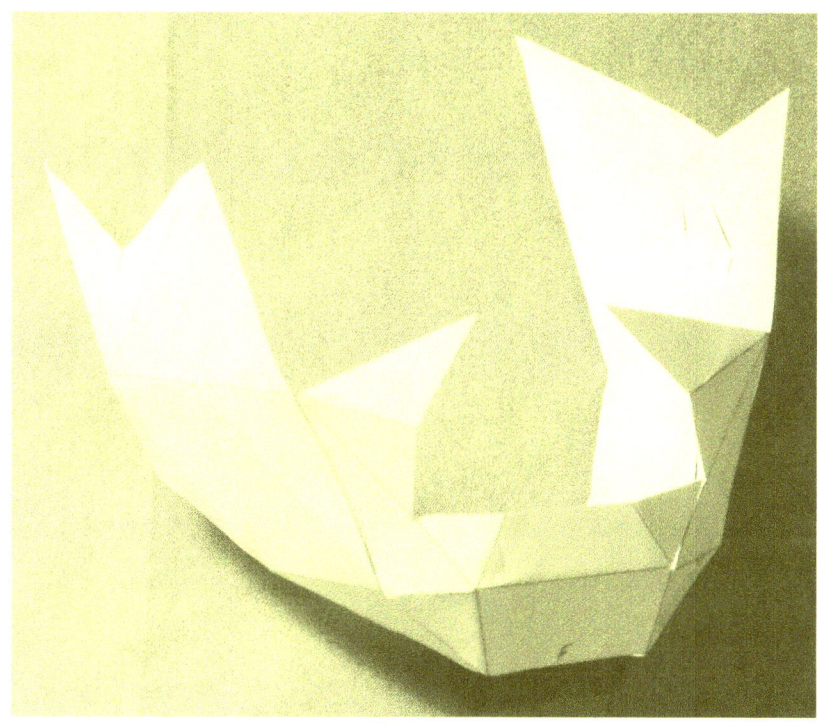

Jaw

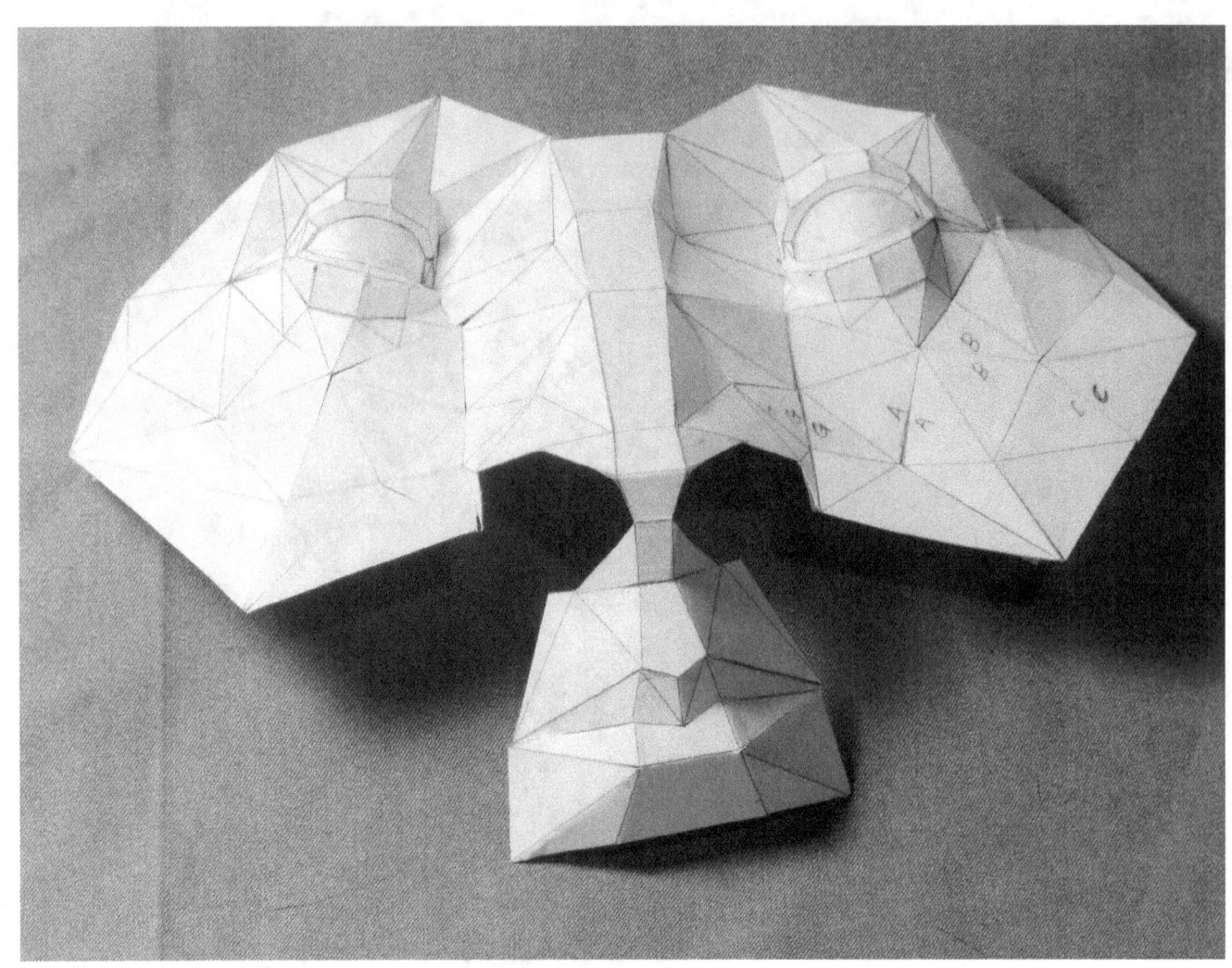

Face

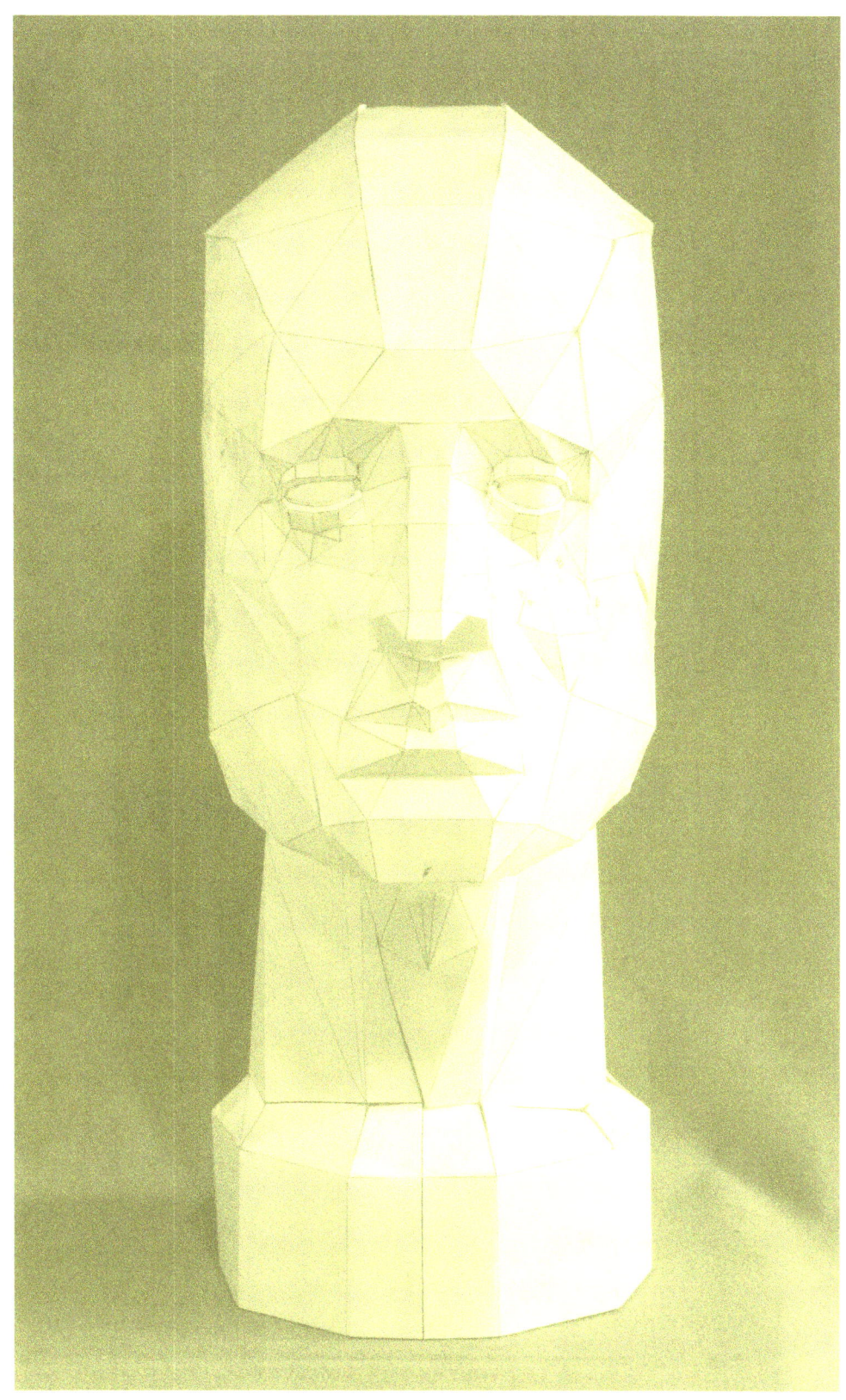

Front View - No Ears

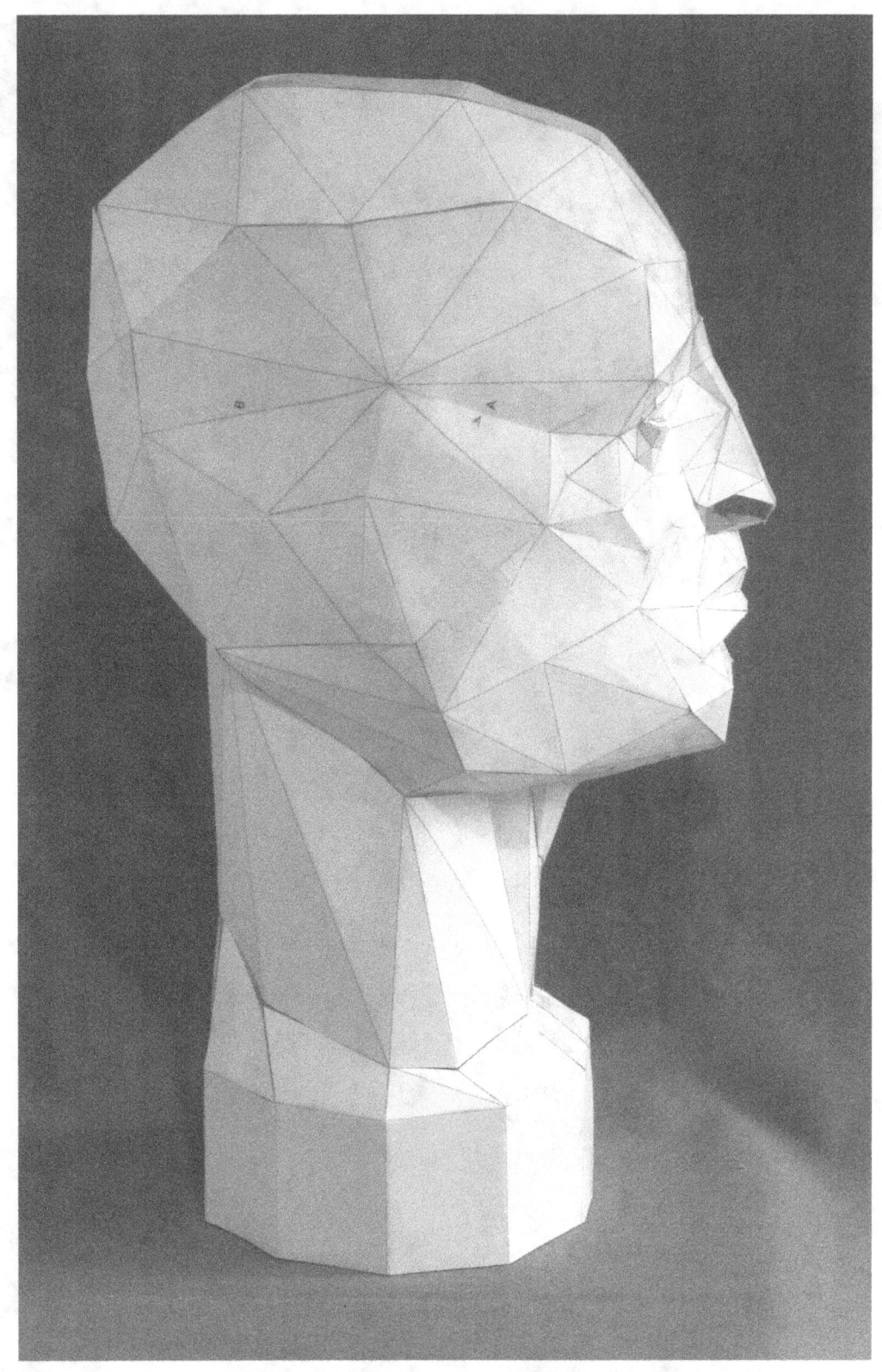

Side View - No Ears

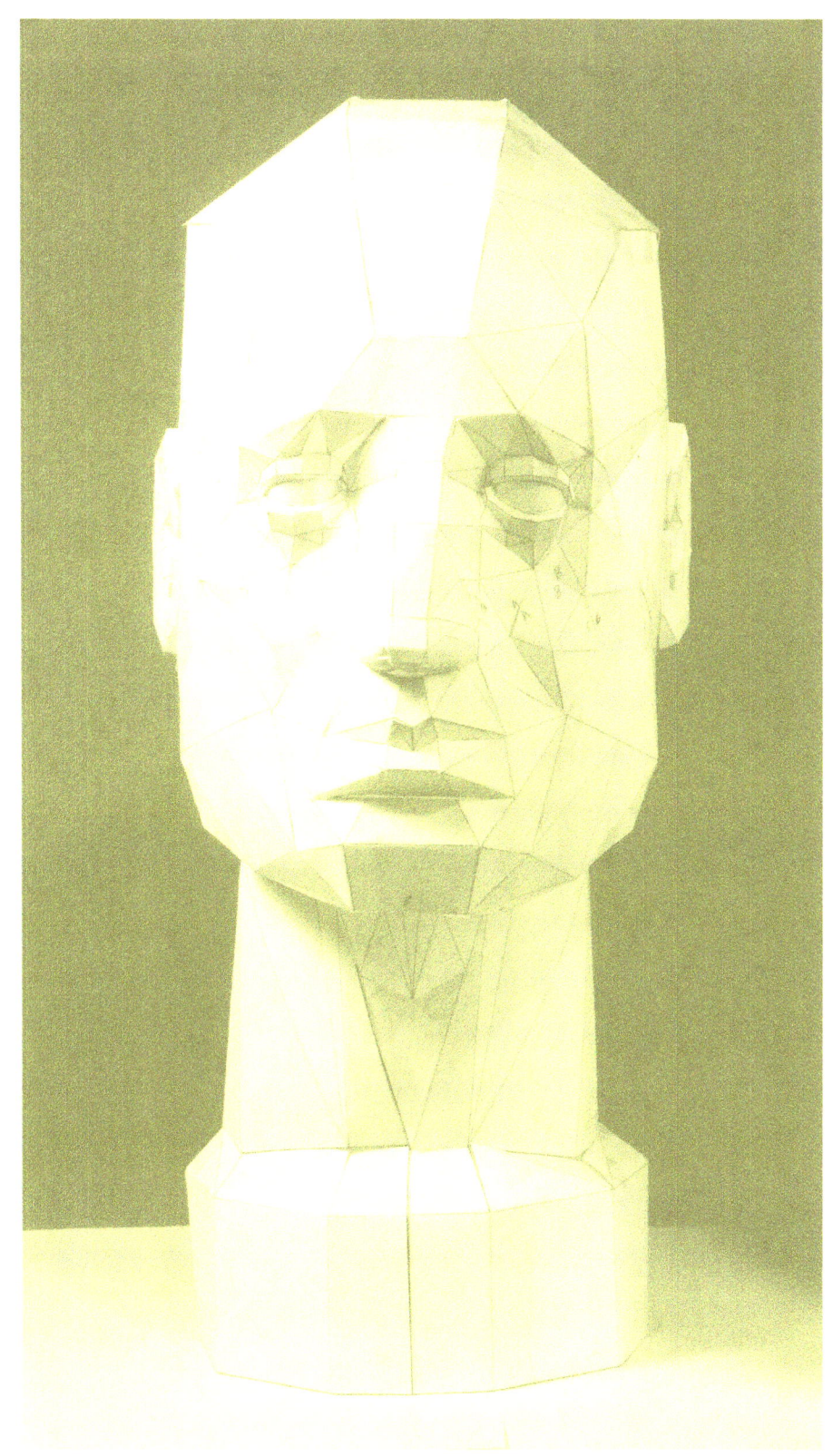

Finished Taping - Front

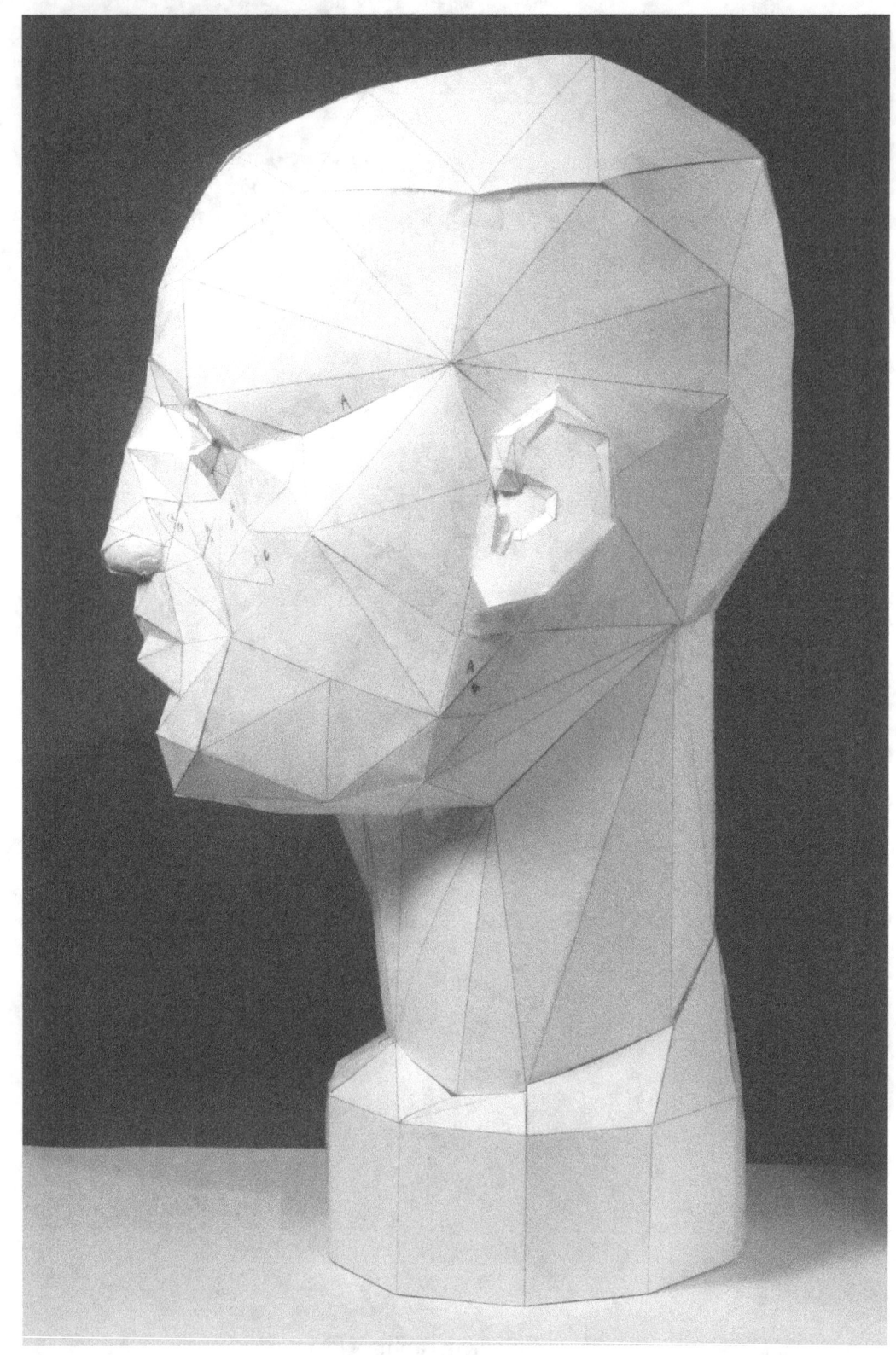

Finished Taping - Side

At this point the head is usable. If you want to make it sturdier and more durable you may want to give it a coat of white acrylic paint, either Titanium White or Gesso will do. This may be followed by a uniform coat of plaster about one eighth inch thick after reinforcing the base with cardboard if you used cover stock as I did. Best to build up several layers. Let it dry completely and sand between layers.

Fill the head with popped polystyrene bean bag refill pellets which can be found at Walmart and elsewhere. Don't confuse with poly-pellets for craft projects. This will stiffen up the head and give it added weight. If you used heavy cardboard you may not need the pellets.

Use the Base Plug pattern to make a part from a 1x6" board, 3/4" thick minimum. Insert the plug and secure with screws. The pattern is 1/8" smaller on all sides to allow for the cardboard reinforcement I used. If your cardboard is thicker adjust the pattern accordingly. Taper or ease the top edge with a rasp or sander for an easy fit.

For plaster I use "Sheetrock" brand joint compound and Utrecht or Winsor & Newton acrylic gesso mixed in a ratio of 2 to 1. These are thicker than other brands and will work better.

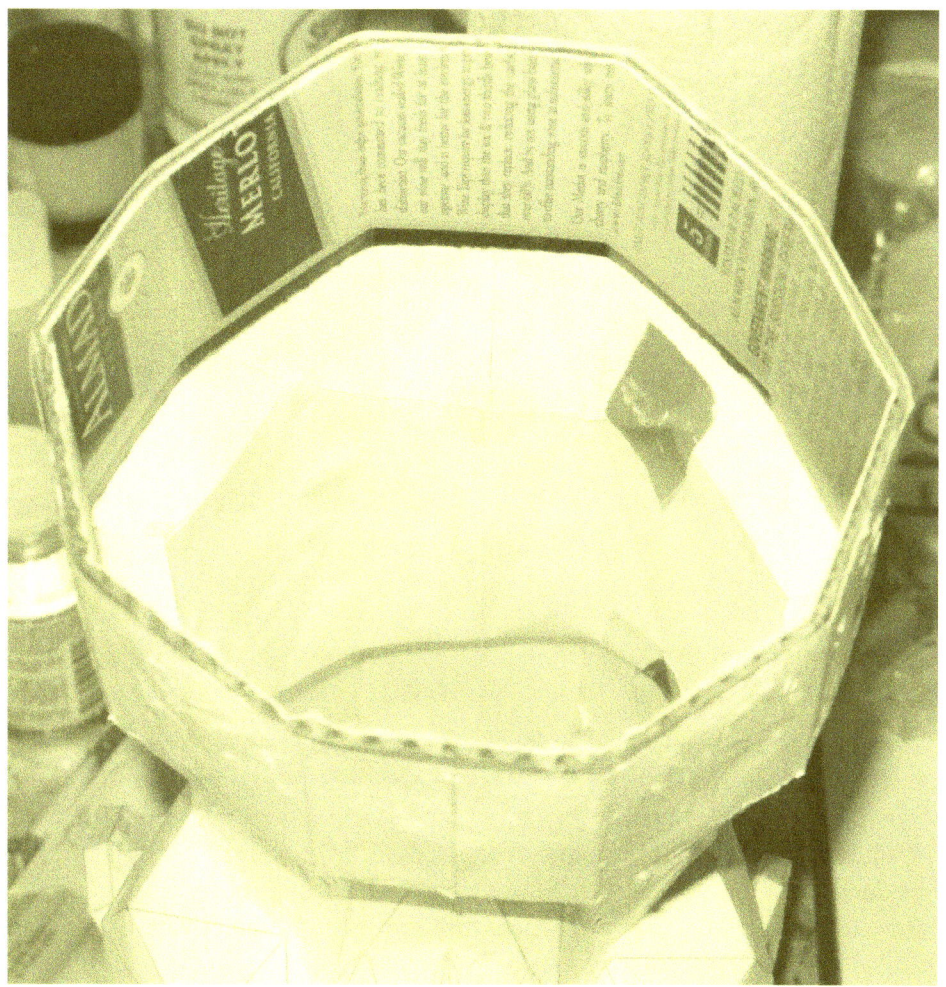

Base reinforced with cardboard and first coat of plaster.

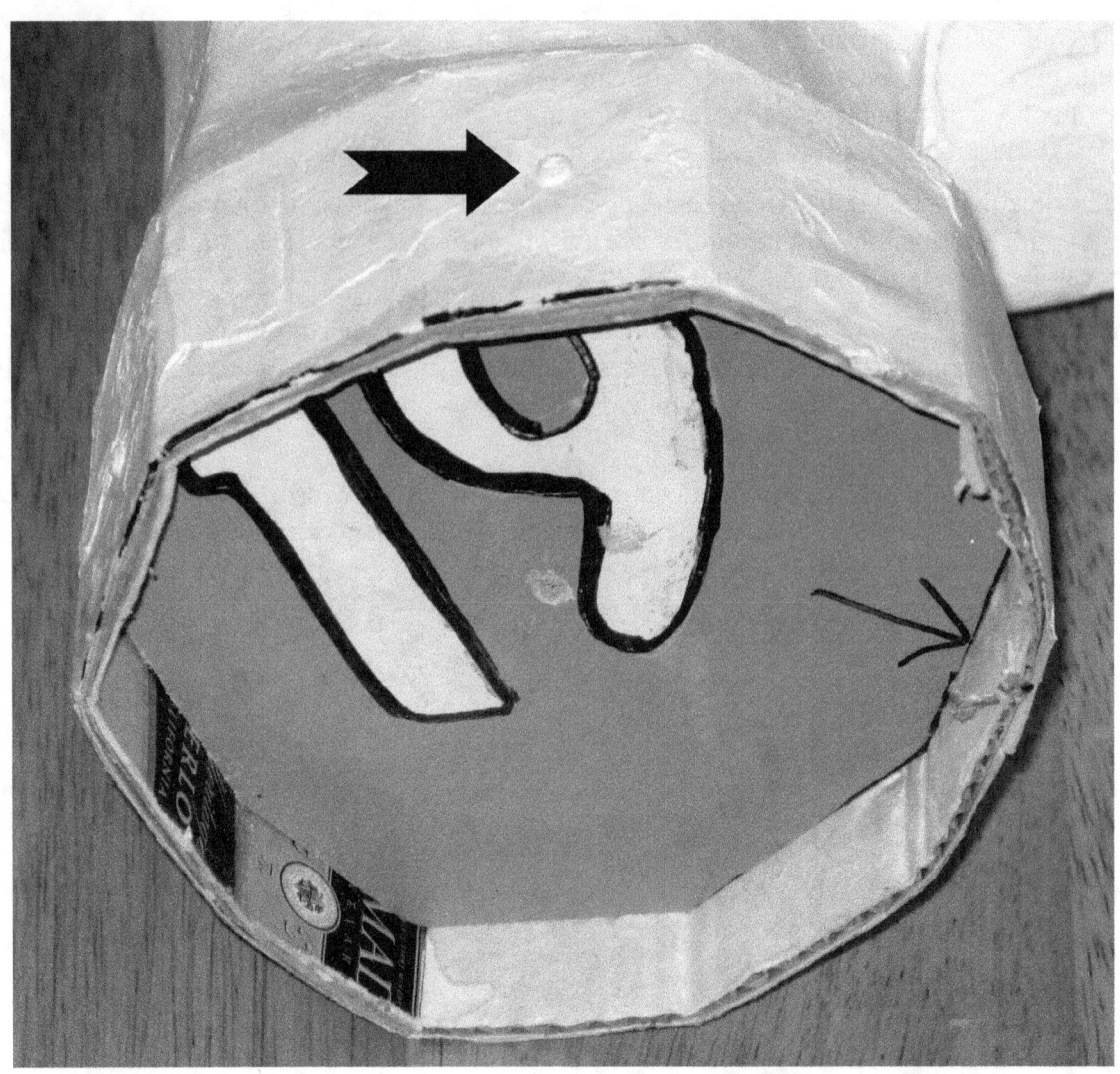

Base Plug & Screws

If you want to enhance or repair your model as I did with the nostrils, Pearl Paperclay mixed with enough glue to make it sticky worked well for me.

Home-made paperclay can also be used. In a large bowl fully soak an entire roll of toilet paper removed from the roll in warm water. Firmly squeeze the water out and press into a measuring cup. You will need 1 1/4 cups. In an empty bowl pull the paper apart into small pieces. Add 3/4 cup of white glue, 1 cup of joint compound, 1/2 cup white flour and 2 tablespoons of linseed oil. Mix well with an electric mixer at least three minutes. Any lumps can be broken up with a fork or fingers. Mix some more. Should make about a quart. Store in an airtight container up to five days or more. The entire model could be covered with this instead of using plaster. It can be sanded and carved when dry.

Thanks to artist Jonni Good for this useful recipe she developed to take the place of paper strips and glue in paper mache sculpture. See her informative website at ultimatepapermache.com. Find her latest book on Amazon.com: How to Make Masks!, and two other books about the art of paper mache.

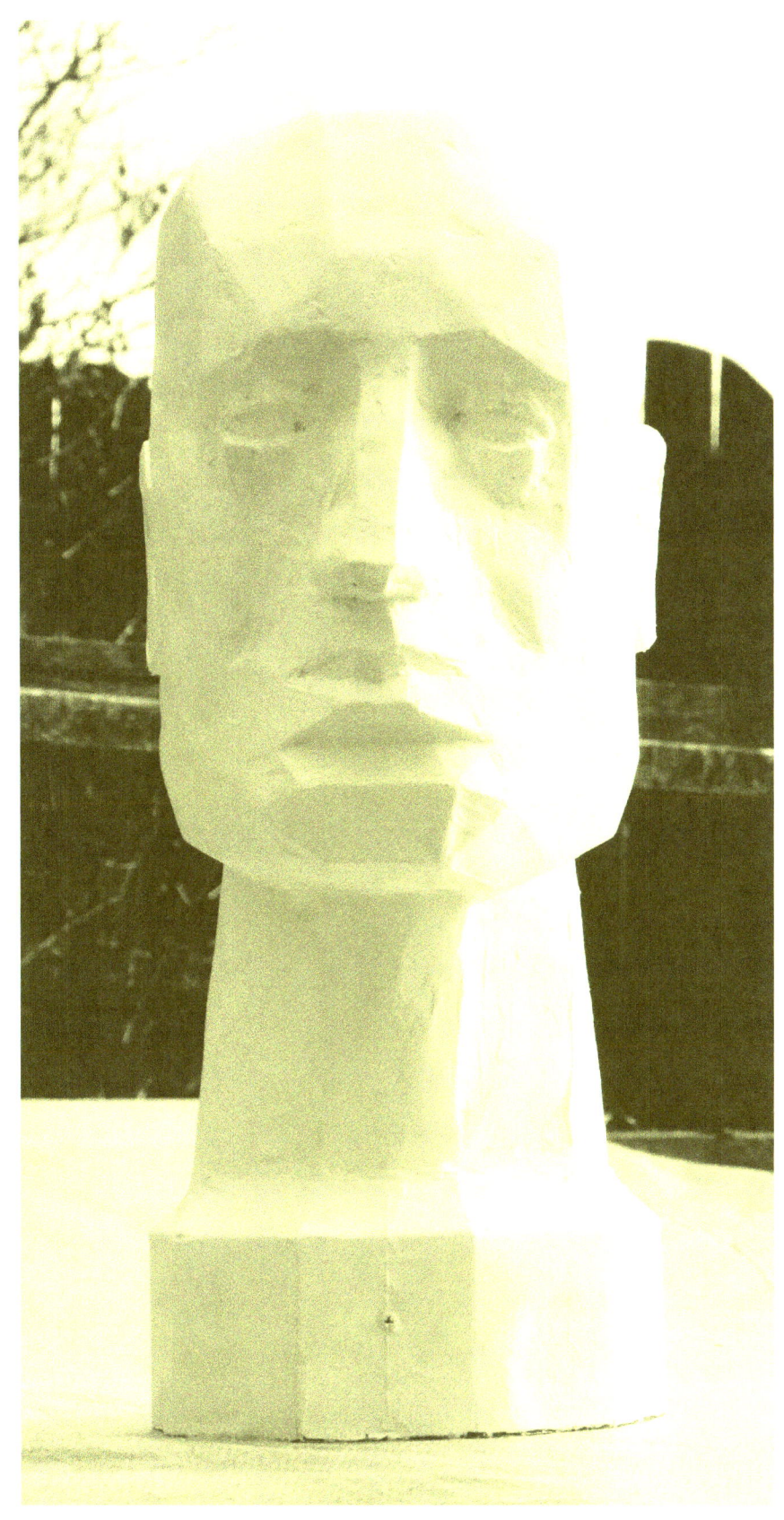

Plastered Head - front

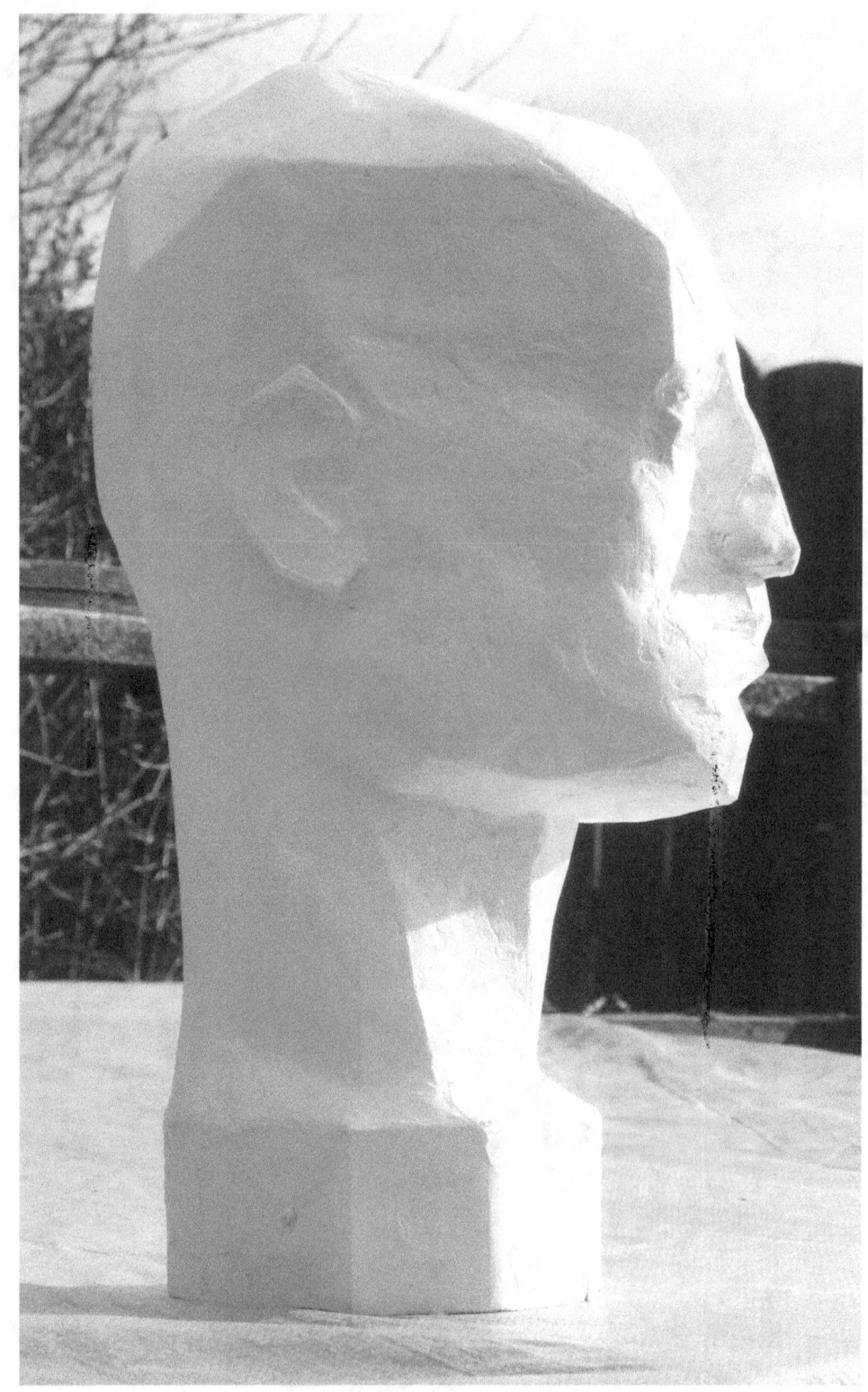

Plastered Head - Side

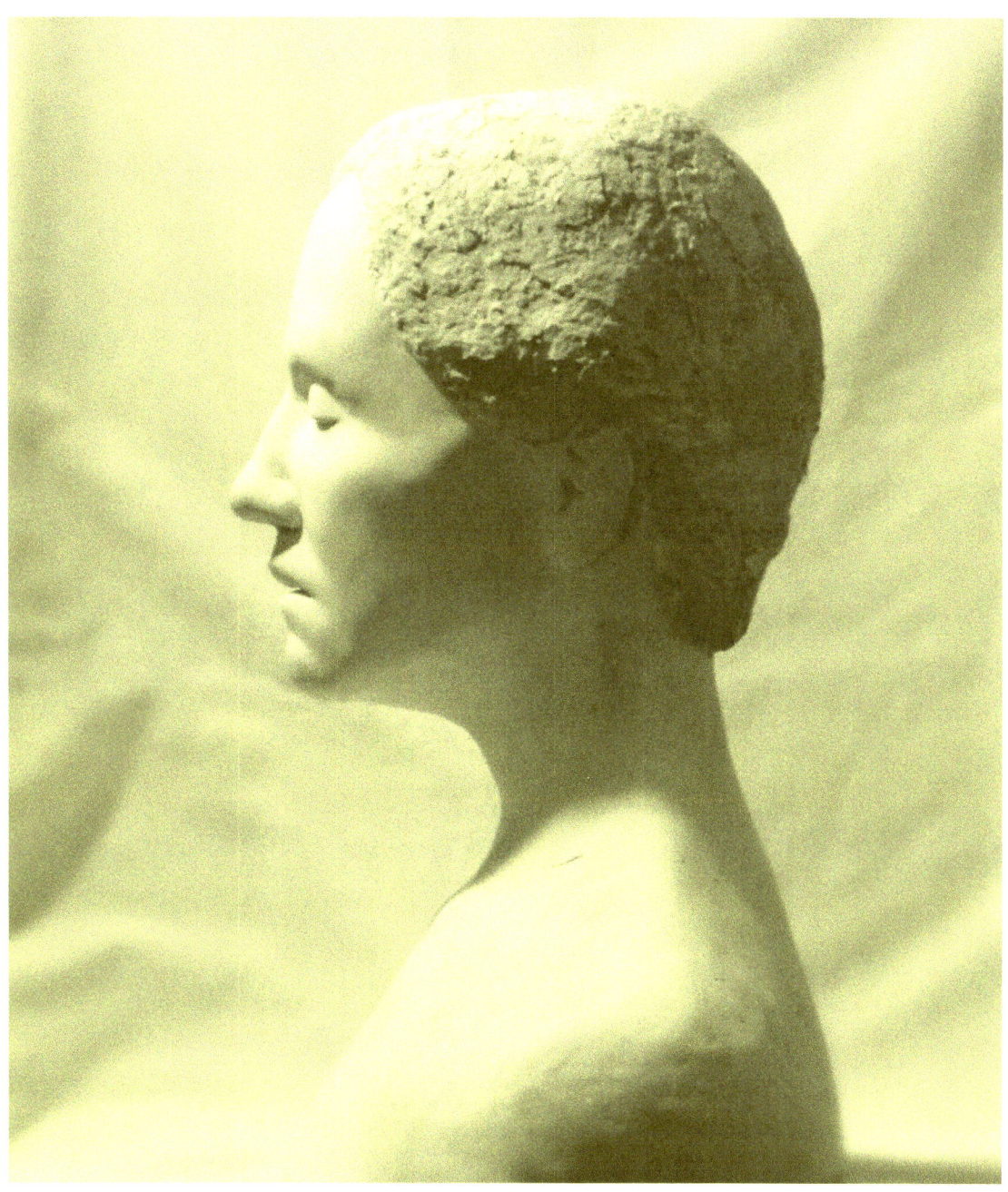

An earlier paper mache bust showing the kind of finish that is possible.

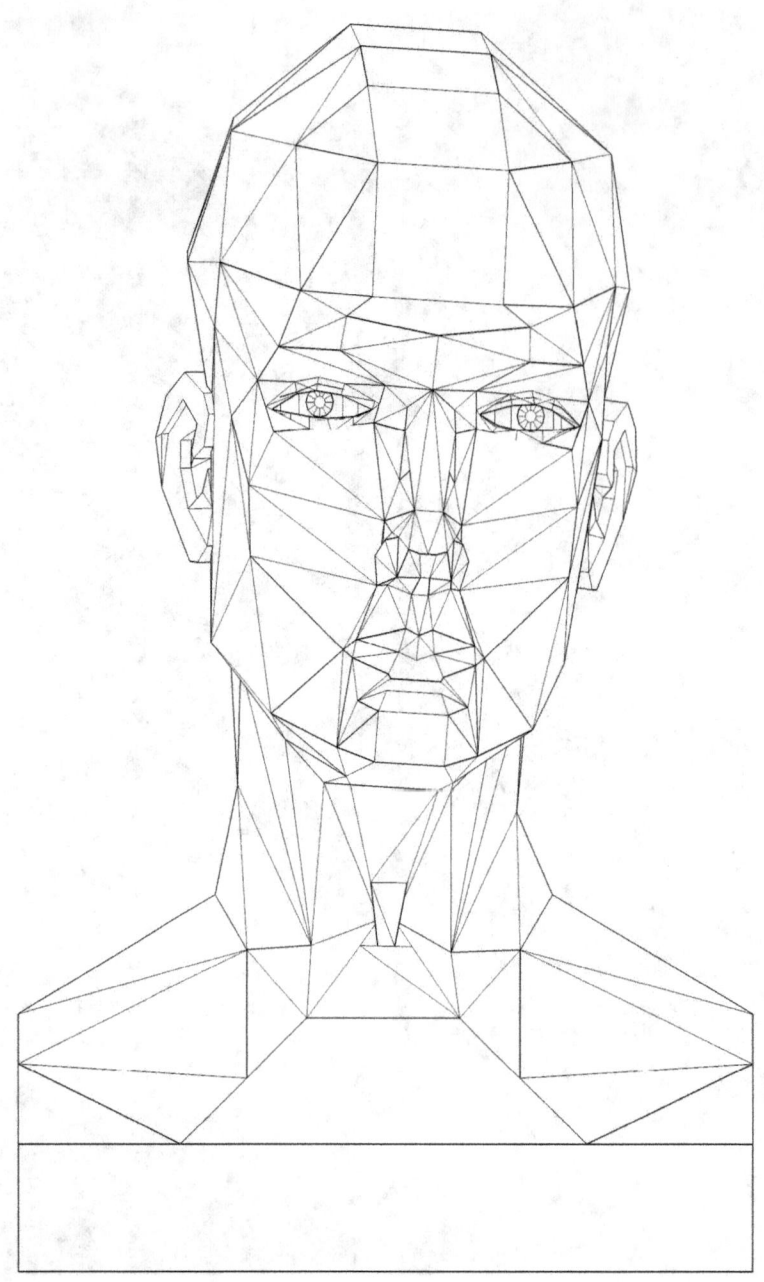

PART 5

Planar Head Two

This one is about a foot high, four inches shorter than the first one.
It looks more feminine, and has a slight tilt to the head and a larger base.

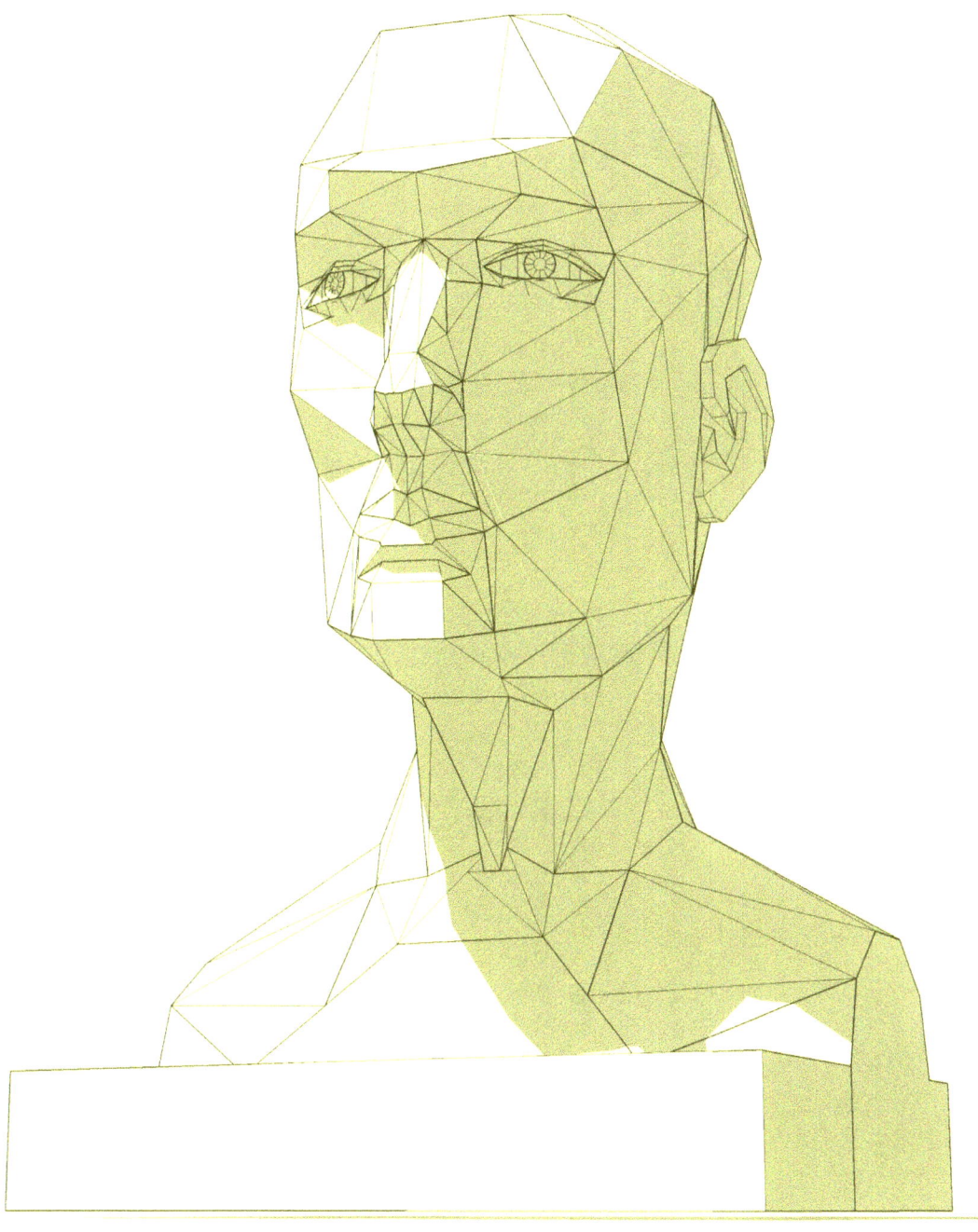

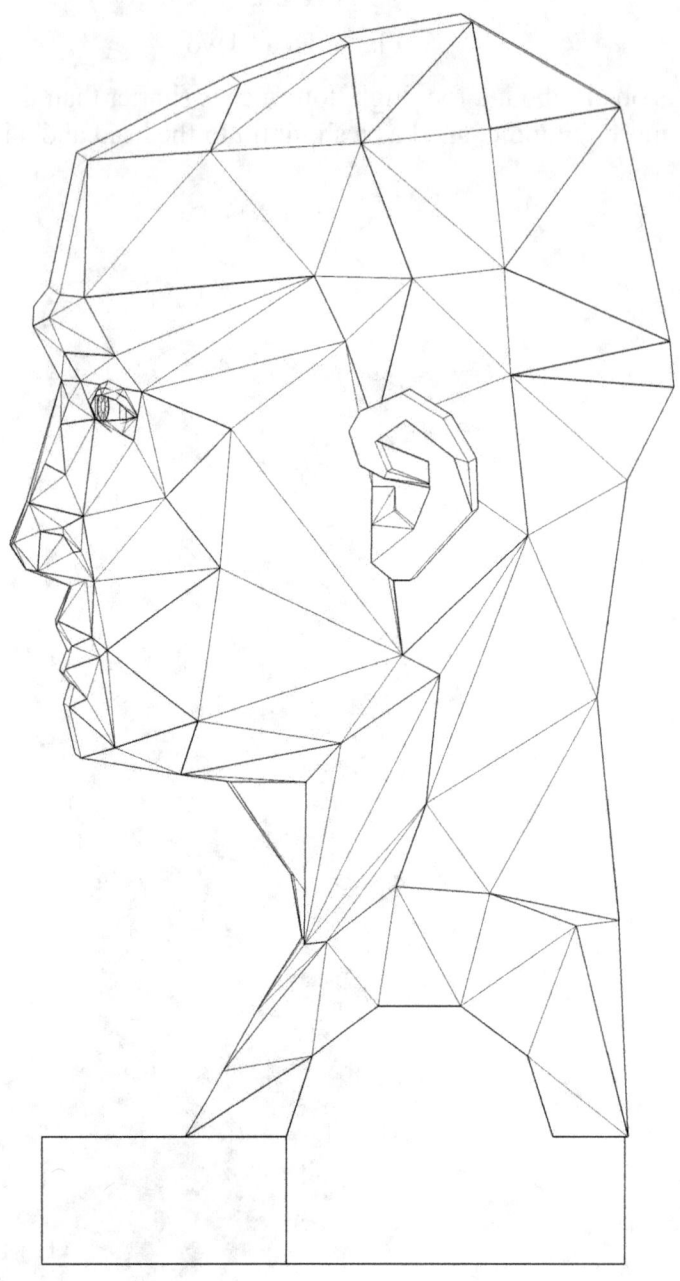

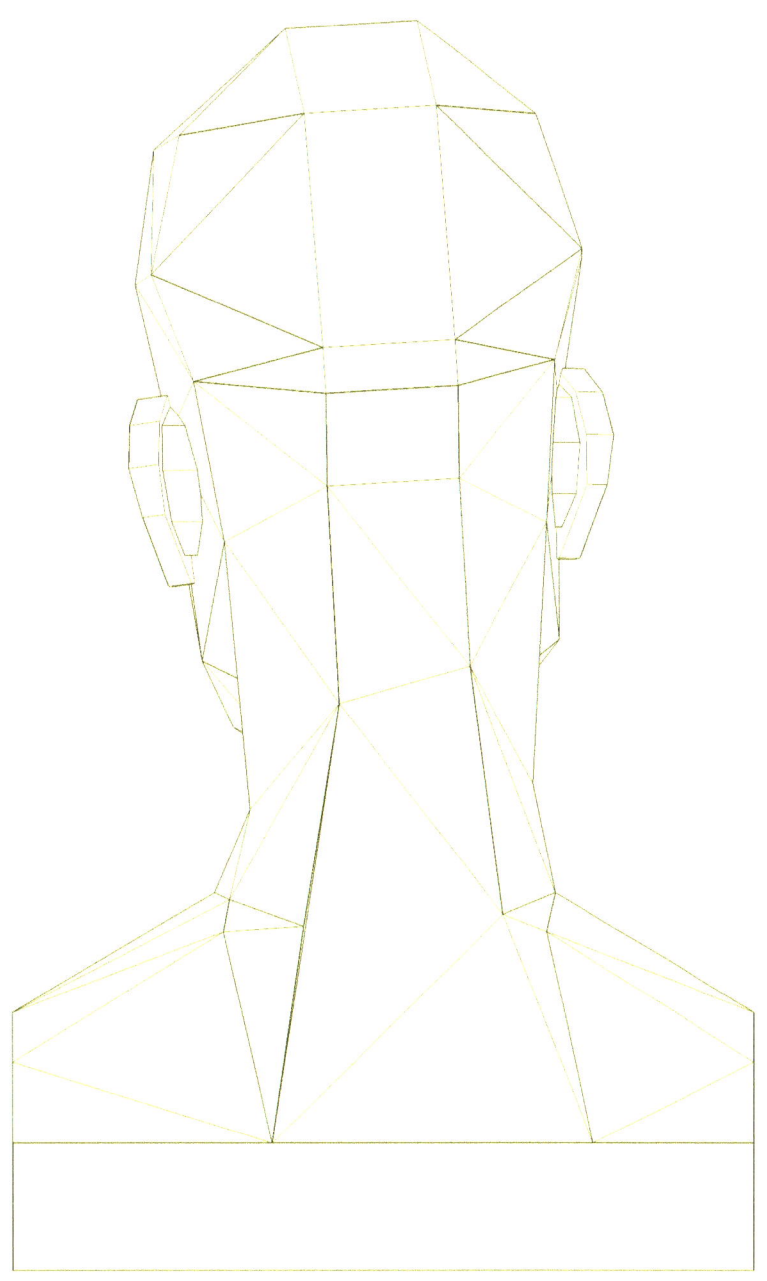

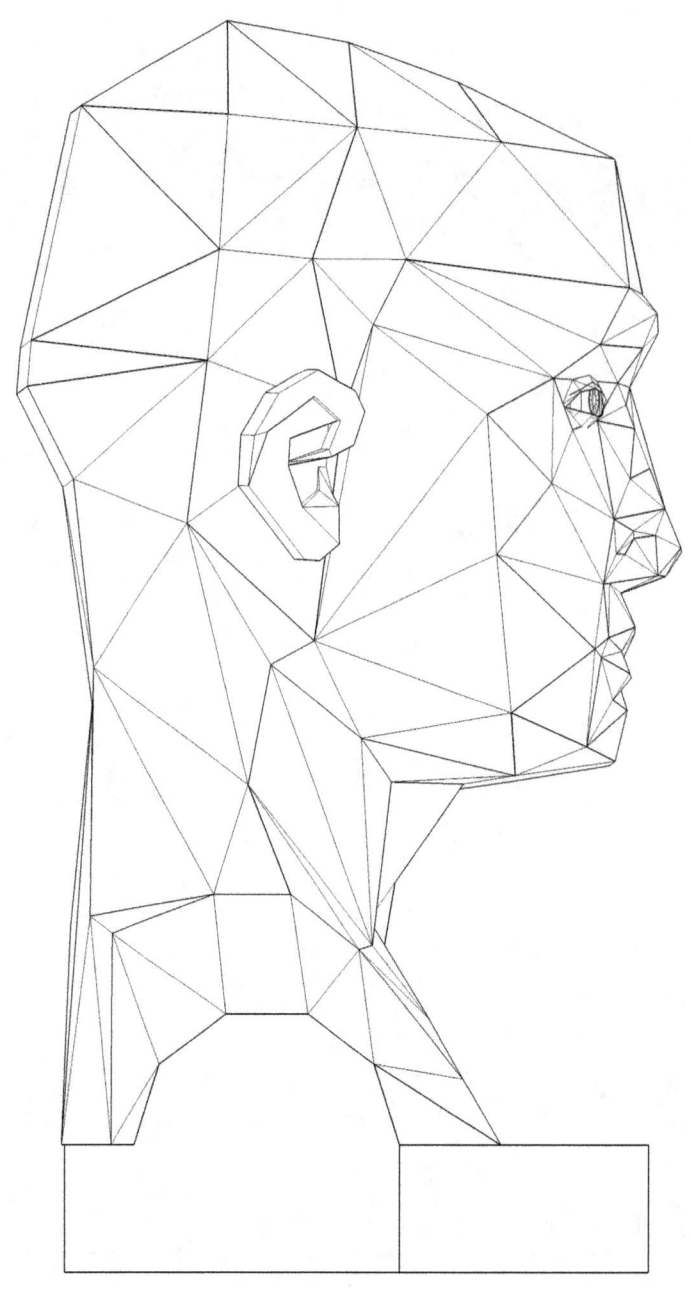

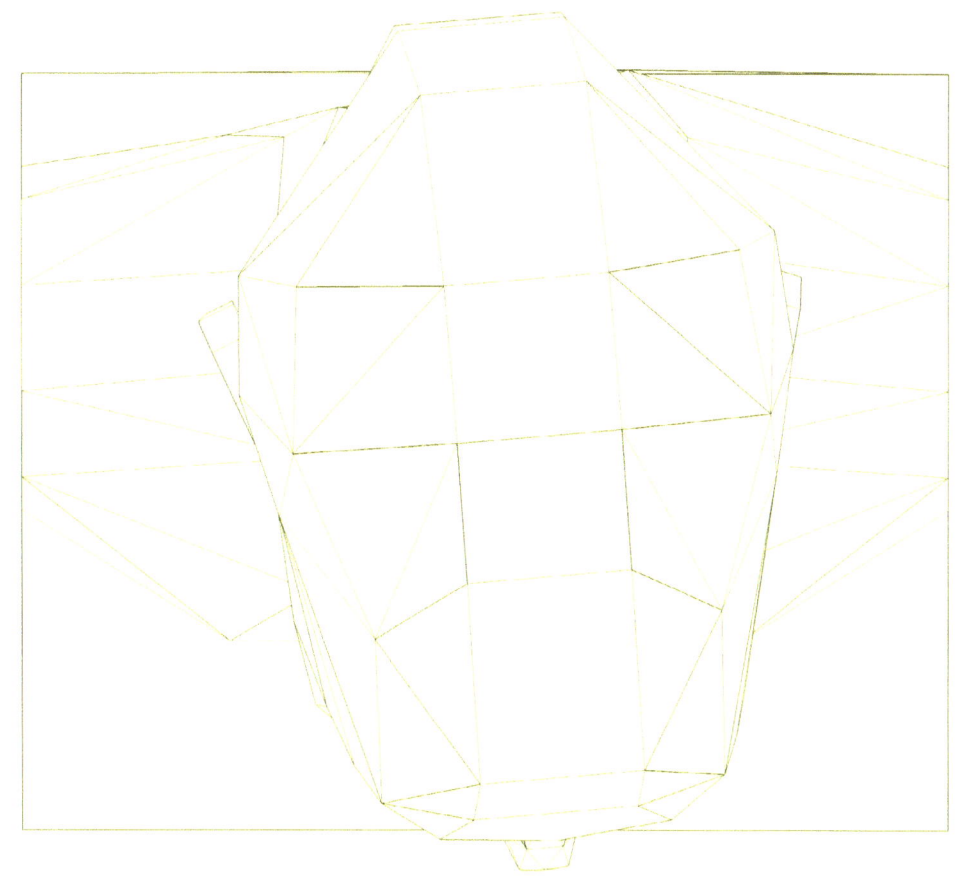

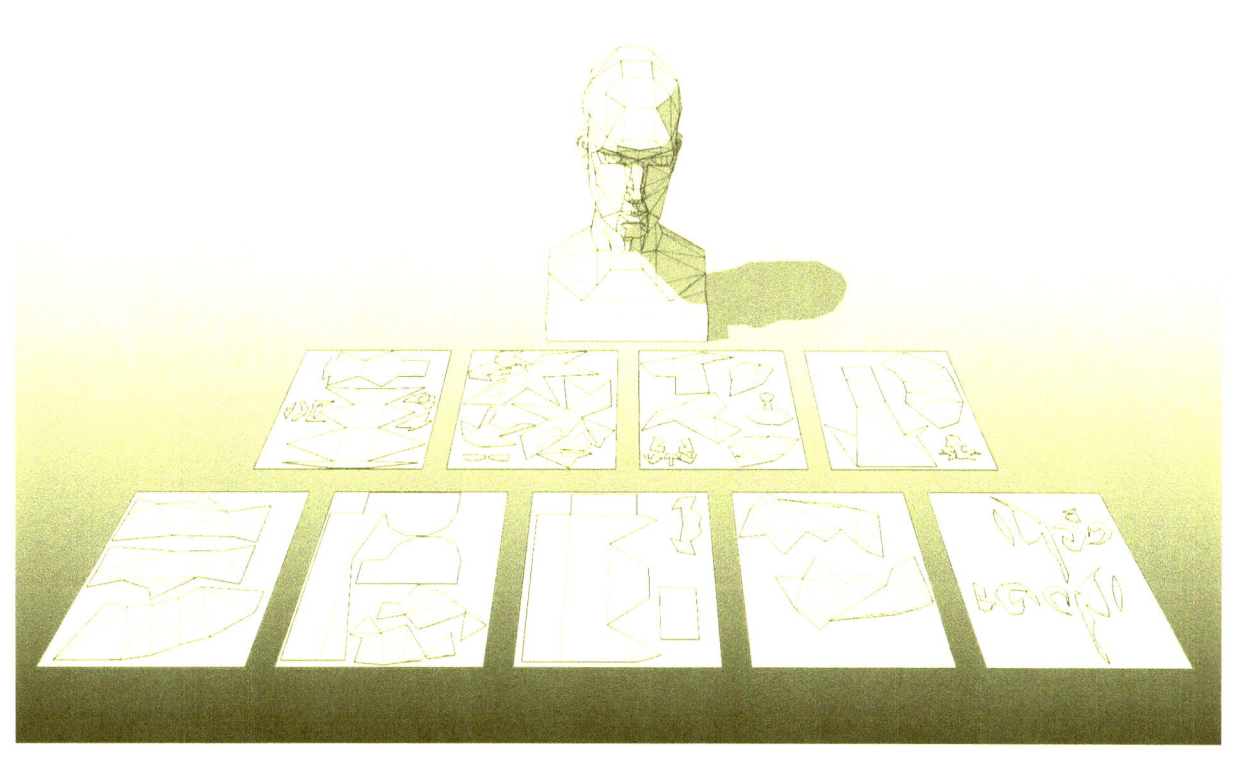

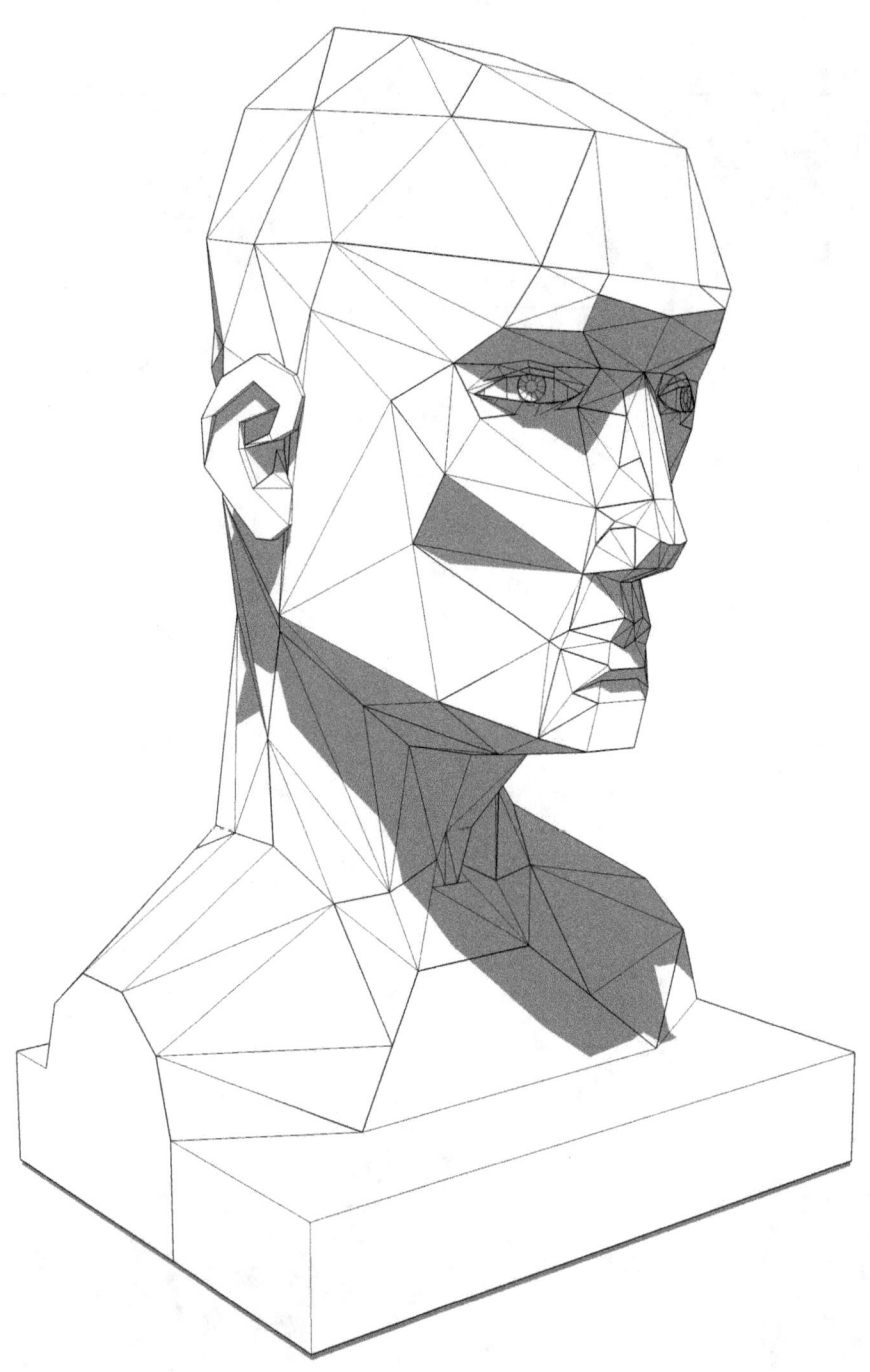

56

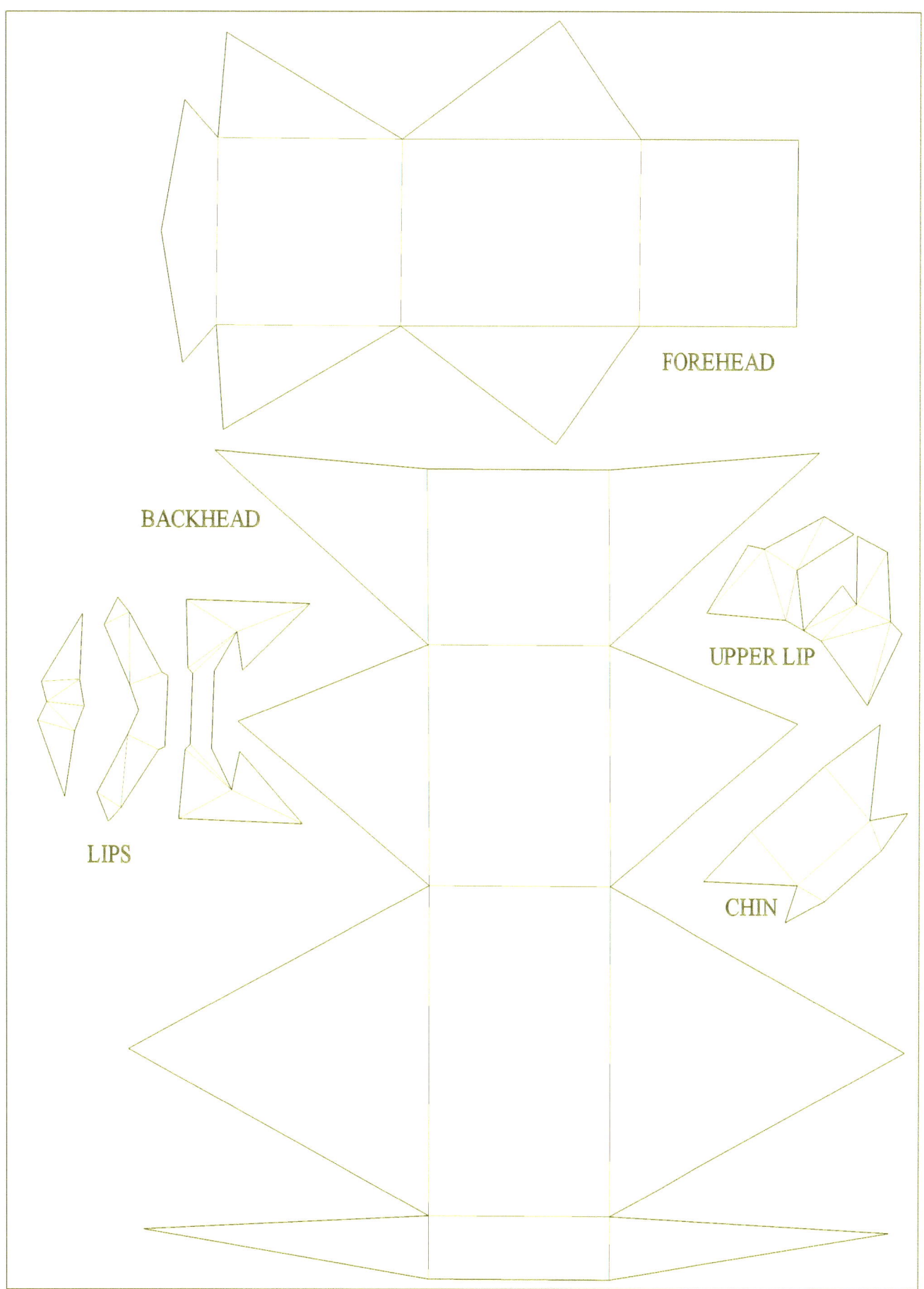

FOREHEAD

BACKHEAD

UPPER LIP

LIPS

CHIN

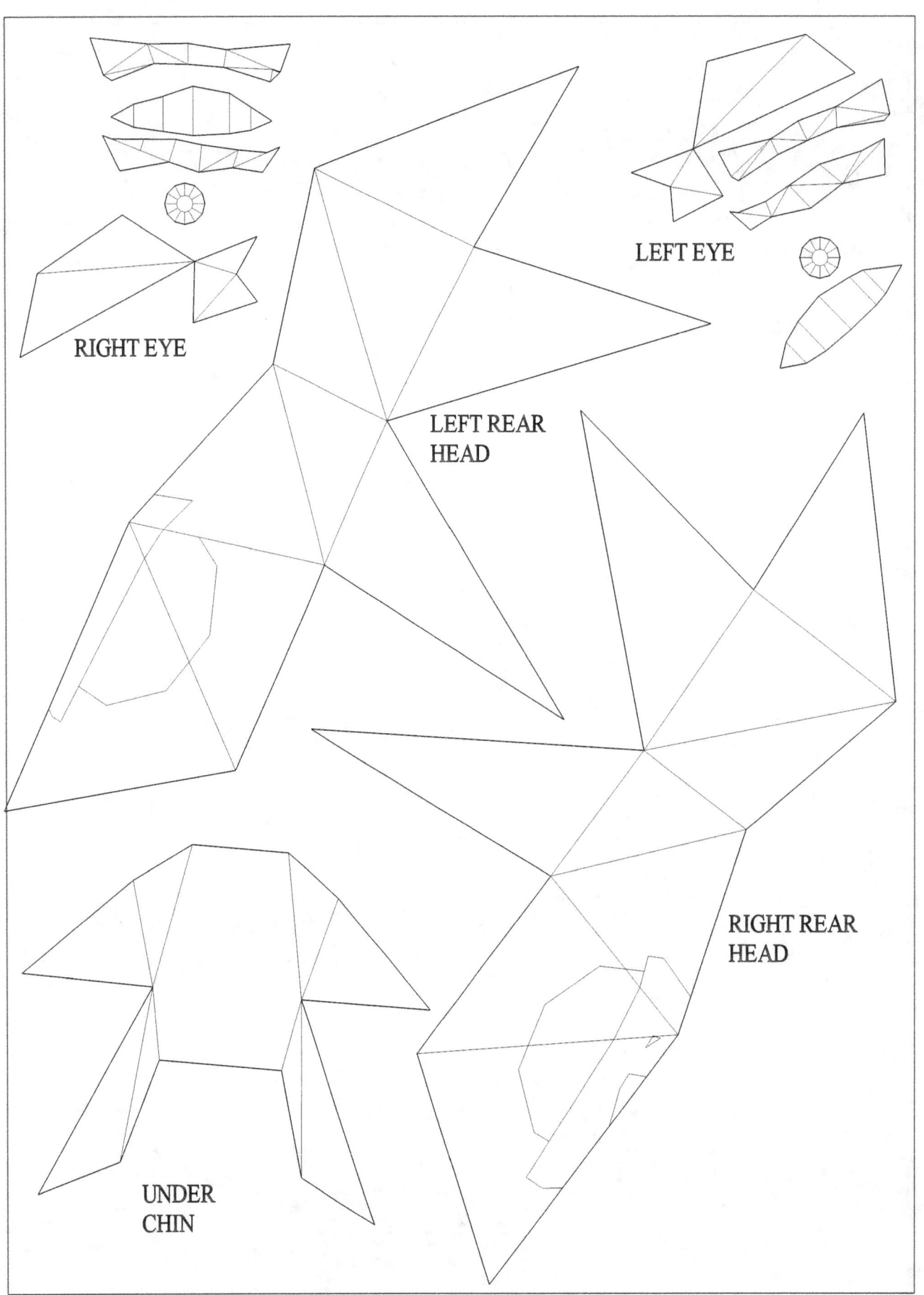

RIGHT EYE

LEFT EYE

LEFT REAR
HEAD

RIGHT REAR
HEAD

UNDER
CHIN

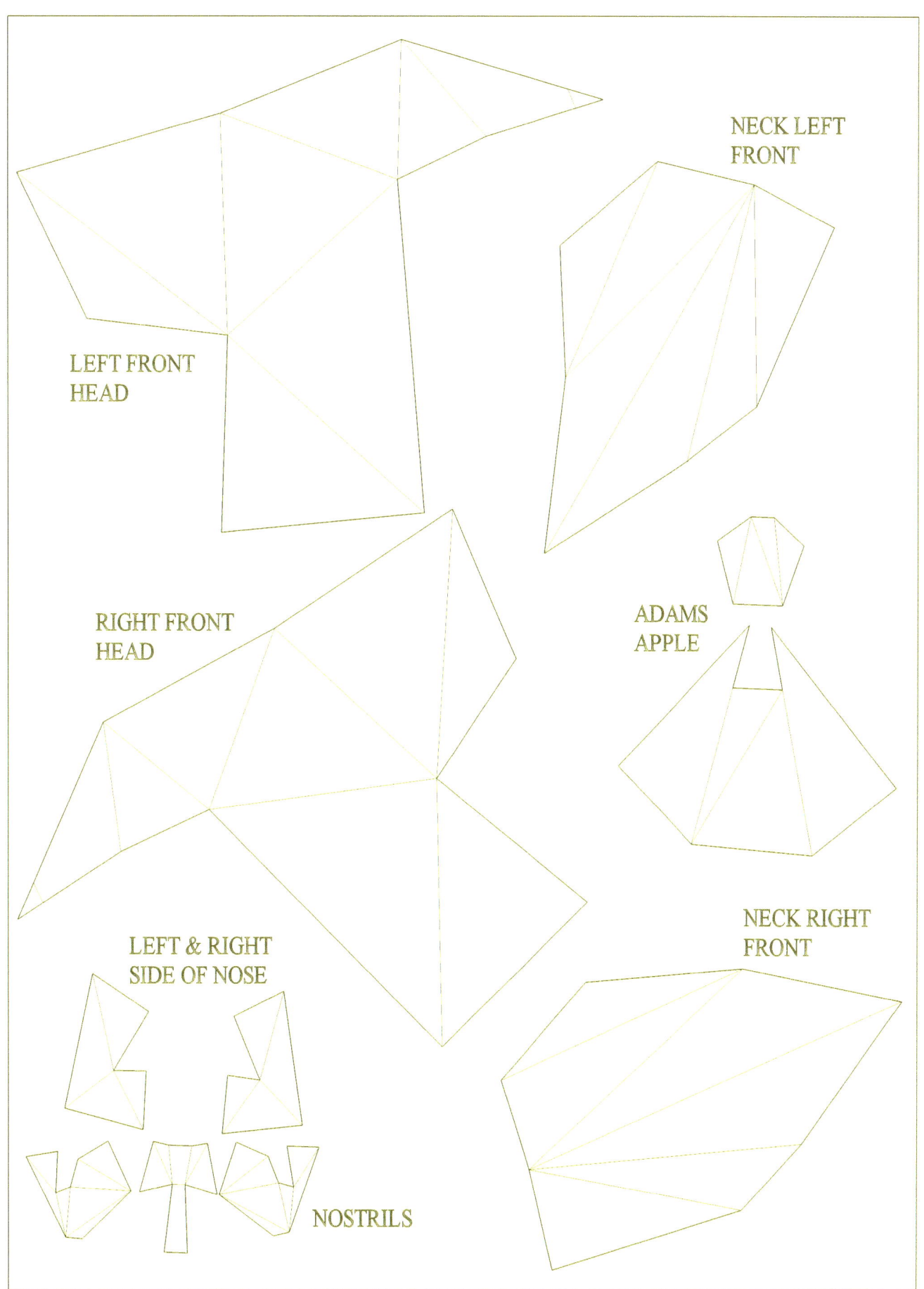

NECK LEFT
FRONT

LEFT FRONT
HEAD

RIGHT FRONT
HEAD

ADAMS
APPLE

LEFT & RIGHT
SIDE OF NOSE

NECK RIGHT
FRONT

NOSTRILS

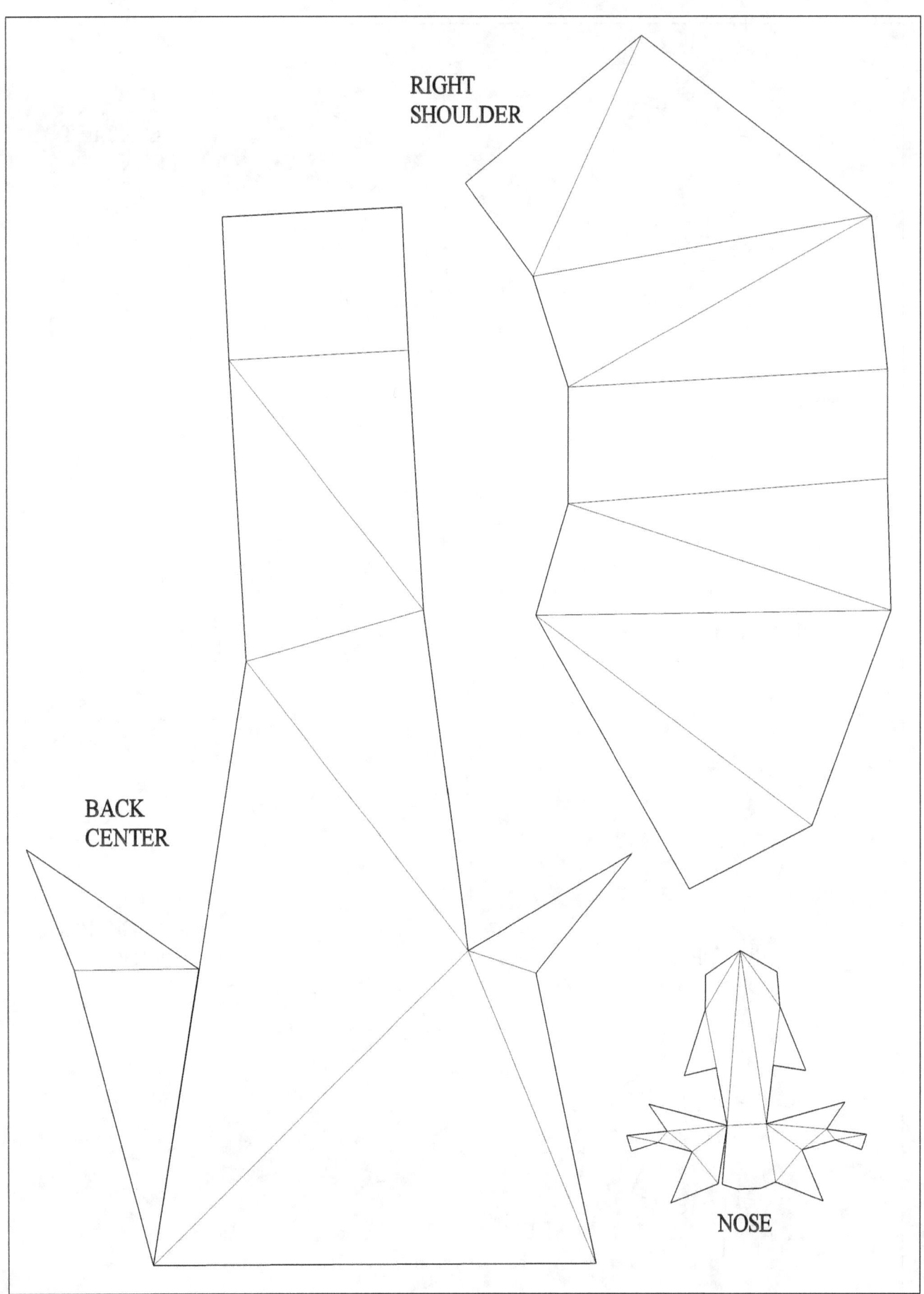

RIGHT
SHOULDER

BACK
CENTER

NOSE

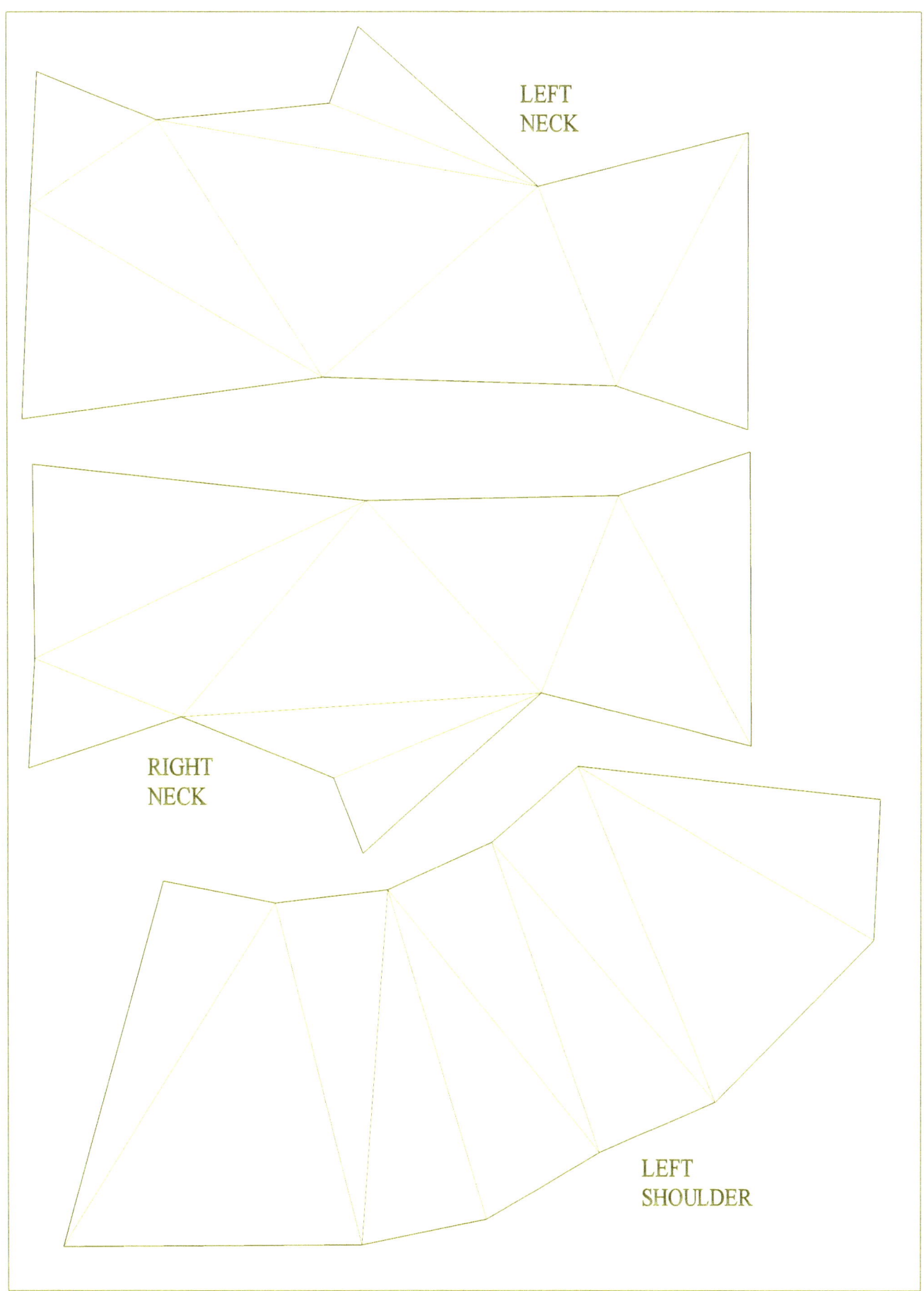

LEFT
NECK

RIGHT
NECK

LEFT
SHOULDER

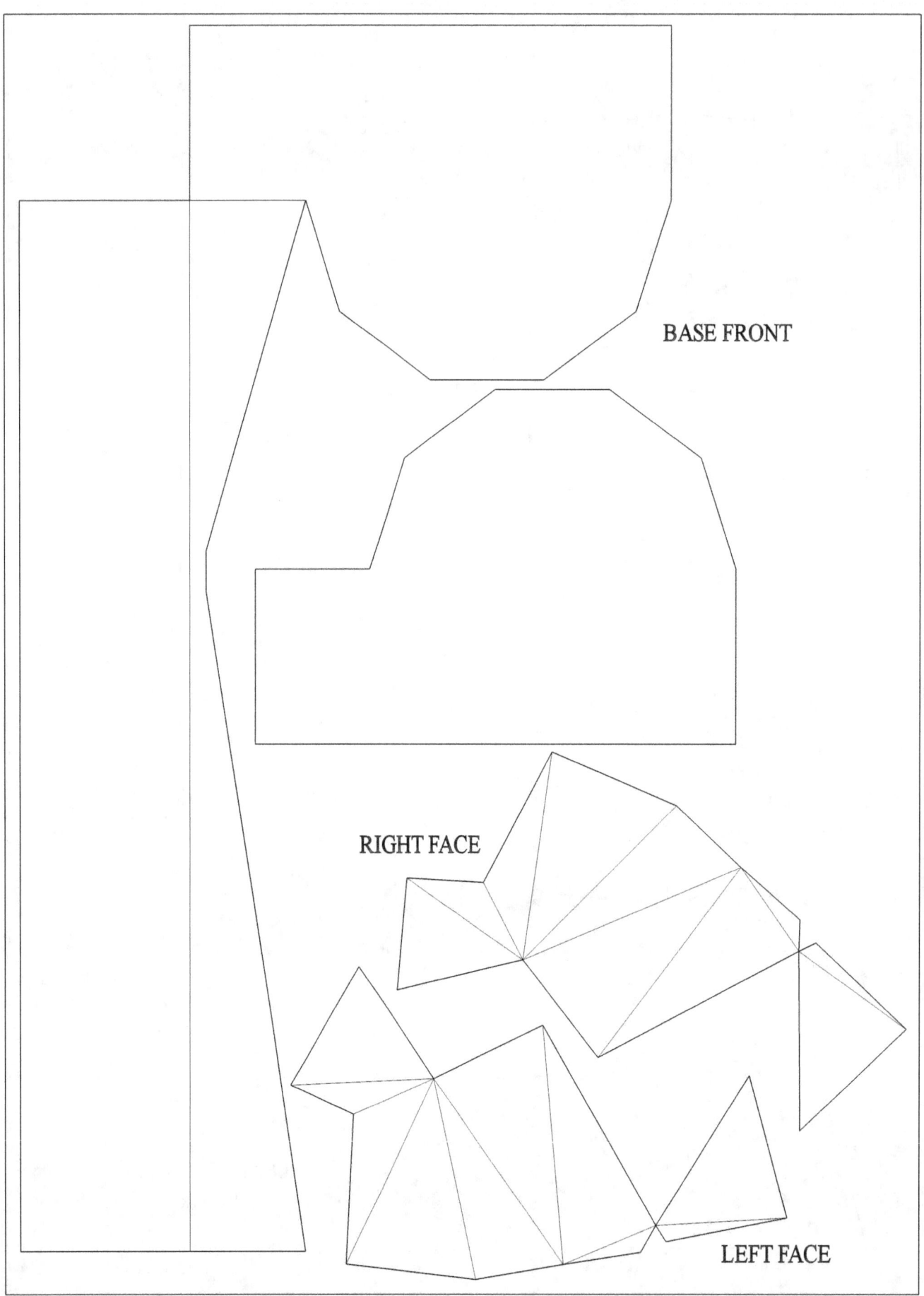

BASE FRONT

RIGHT FACE

LEFT FACE

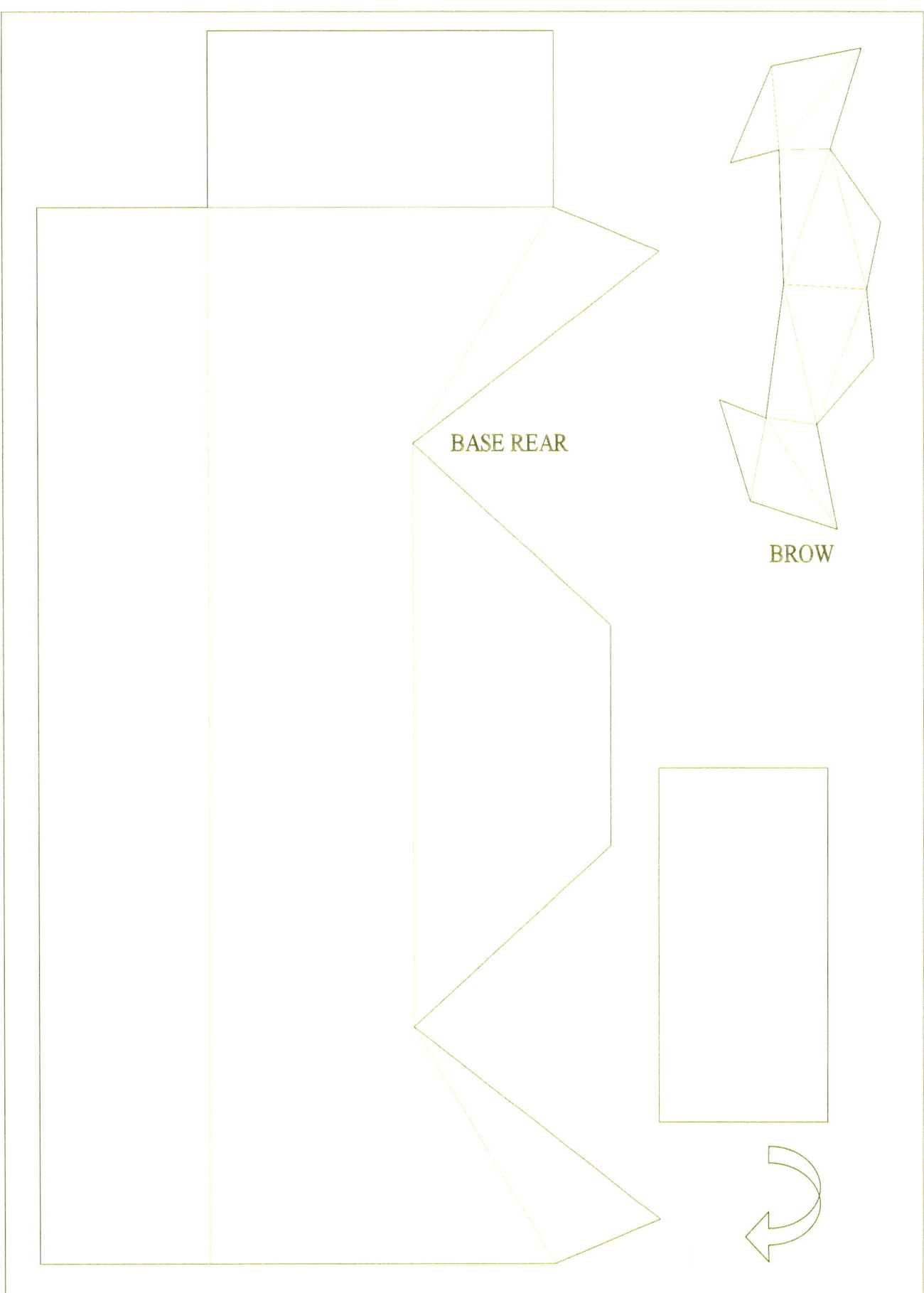

BASE REAR

BROW

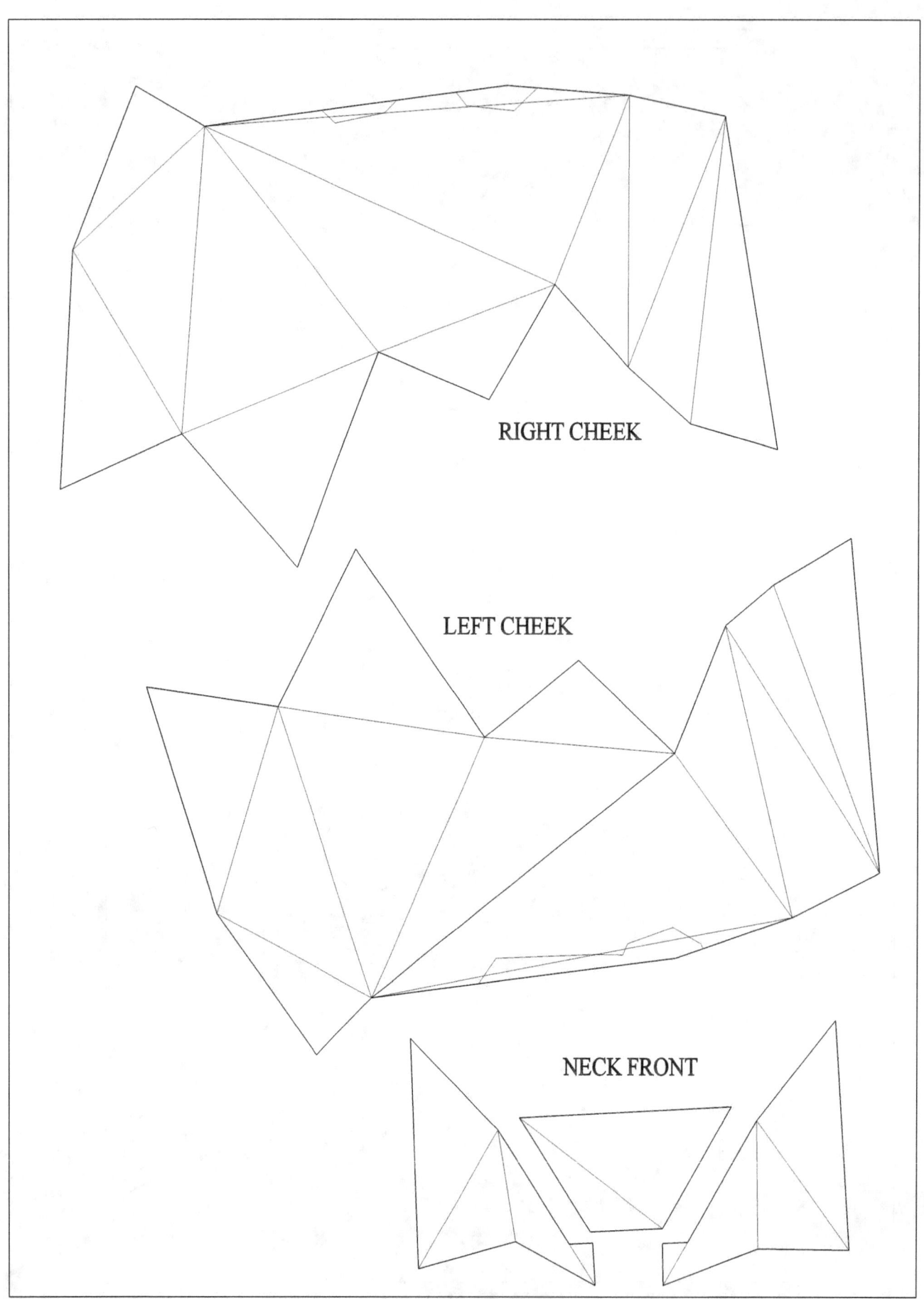

RIGHT CHEEK

LEFT CHEEK

NECK FRONT

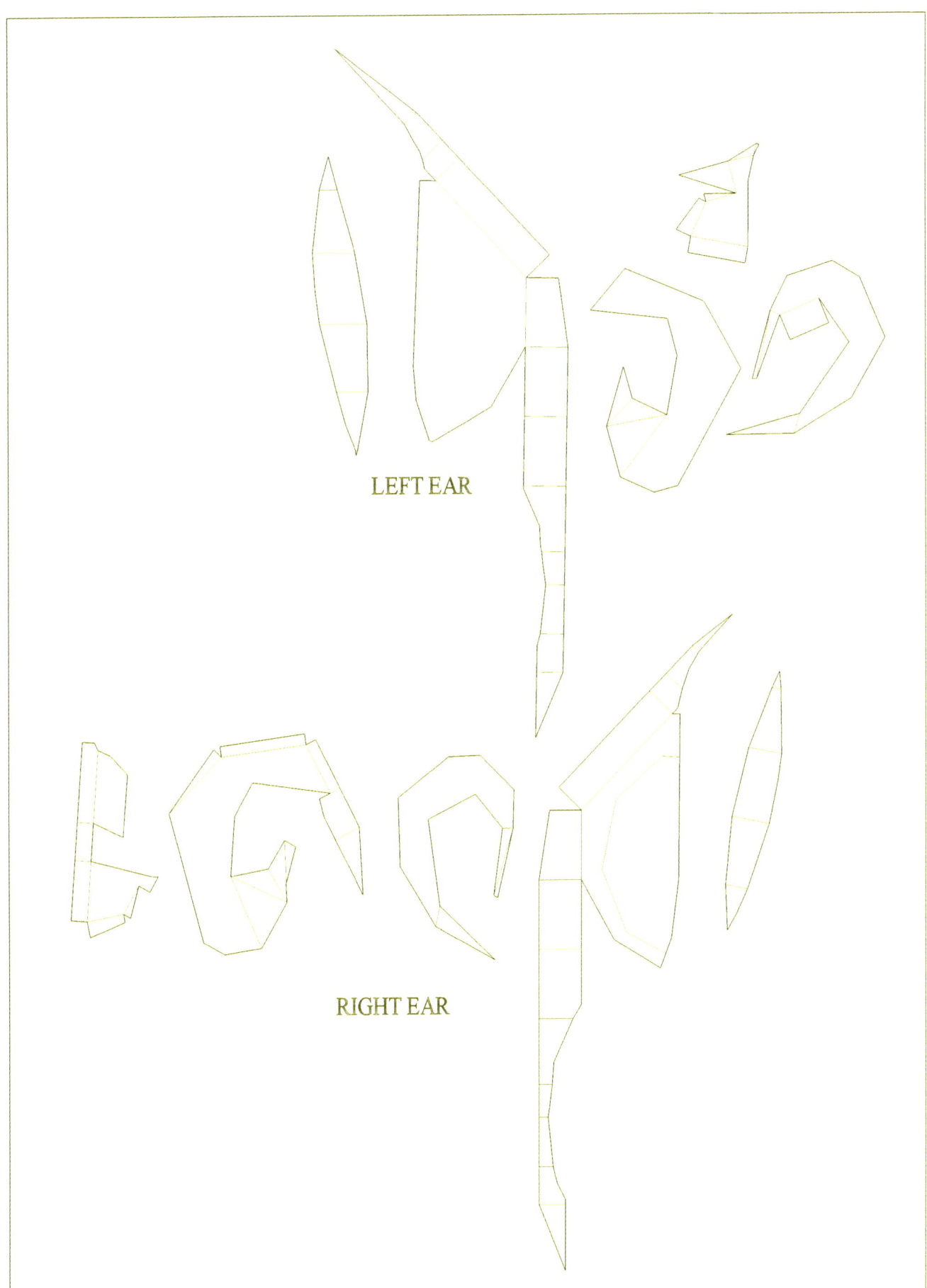

LEFT EAR

RIGHT EAR

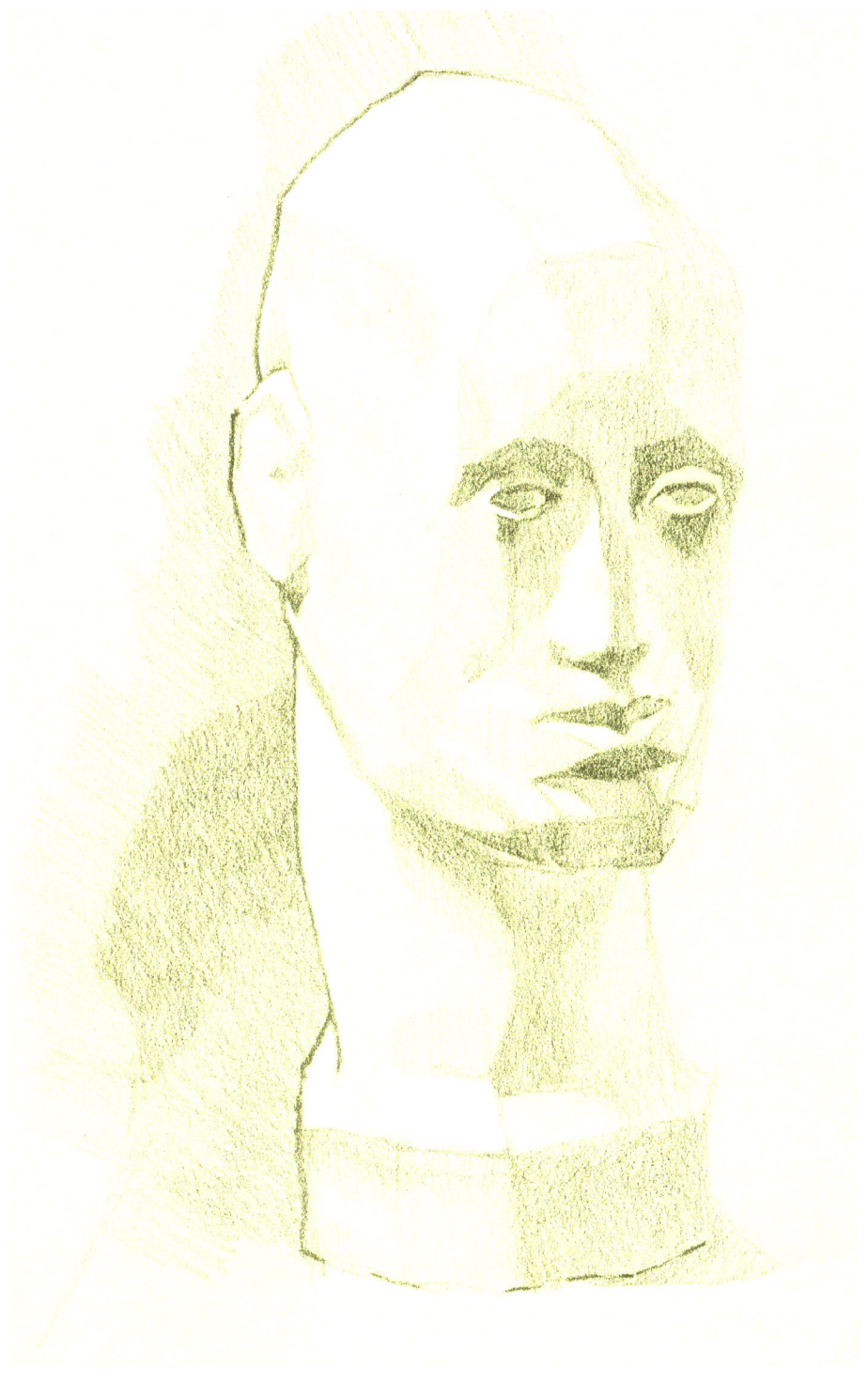

A sketch from the Planar Head, on white sketchbook paper scanned into the computer. In PaintShop I darkened the drawing so it looks like it was done on light gray paper. With the Density and Opacity set to lower levels I made stokes that resemble white pastel pencil for the highlights.

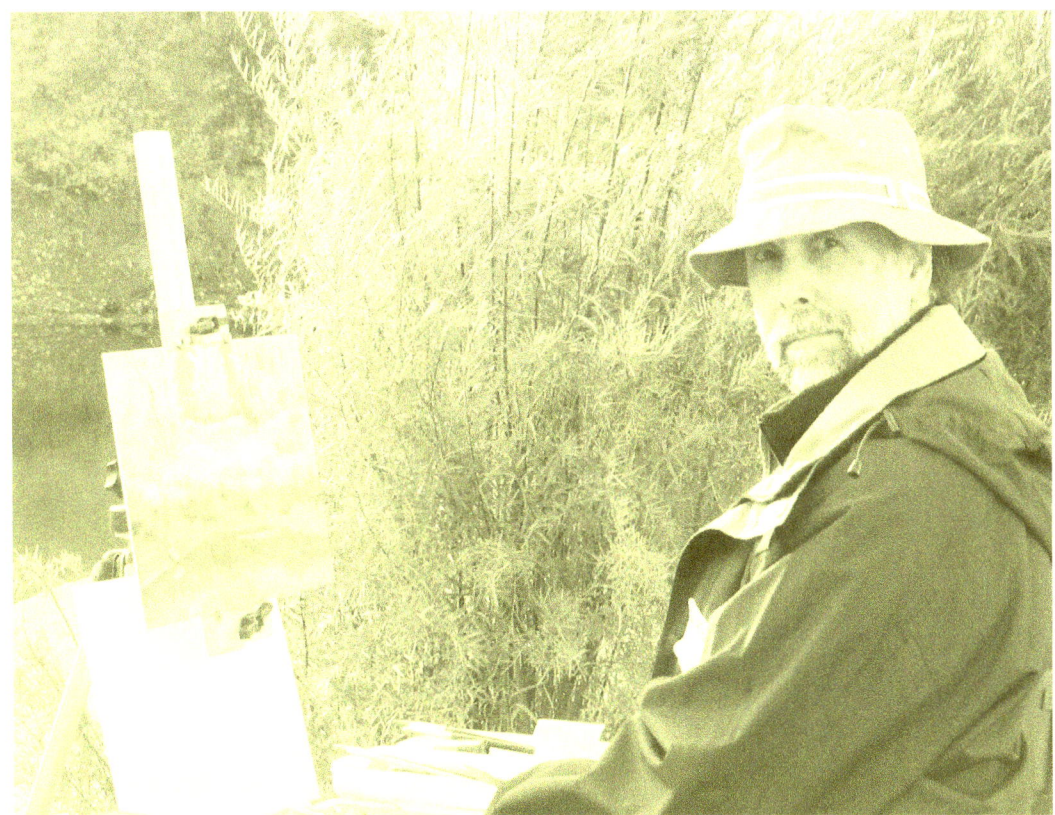

Hope you enjoy making these models and increasing your understanding of the human head in the process. Your ability to draw and paint from life and from photos should improve if you spend time drawing and painting from these models. Vary the lighting and point of view. And they make interesting art objects for the home or studio.

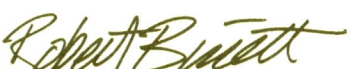

Stop by my extensive website when you have time: robertbissett.com or buildart.com.

High quality archival prints of my work can be found at http://robert-bissett.artistwebsites.com/.

About the author: Artist, Teacher, Author, Blogger, Architectural Designer

Born in Little Falls, New York, 1945, Robert Bissett is known for exceptional portraits and plein-air and studio landscapes. He was featured in the 1995 North Light book, Acrylic Painting Techniques, therein recognized as a master artist. He is a workshop teacher and author of two books on art.

He graduated from the Air Force Academy in 1967, served over five years as a pilot including two tours in Viet Nam. Returning to school after the service he graduated from Washington State University with a degree in architecture, Summa Cum Laude.

A career in architecture seemed more practical, but the urge to paint became overwhelming in the summer of 1980. That fall he had his first show at a gallery in Anchorage, Alaska. Most of the paintings were landscapes and it sold out. The following spring a mountain "portrait" was selected as the subject for a four thousand edition Beautiful Alaska promotional print, 16" x 48". Bissett moved to Idaho in 1980. He has traveled throughout the US, Japan, Australia, Spain, Turkey, Ethiopia, Greece, Iran, Greenland, England, Puerto Rico, Mexico, Costa Rica and Italy. His paintings are a valued part of many private collections.

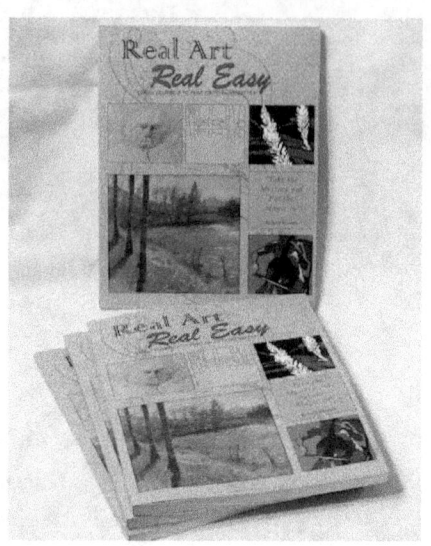

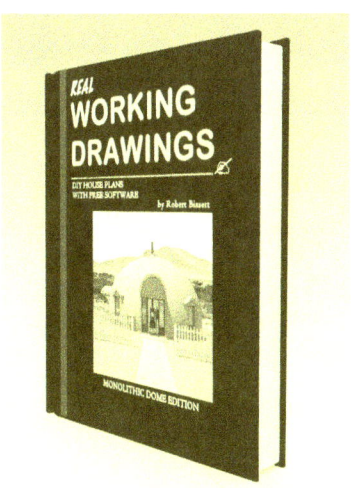

DIY House Plans Using Free Software

Not just for domes,

Applicable to any construction style

Takes the reader through all the stages required to produce a functional and attractive set of working drawings. The prospective home owner will learn how to start with a pencil-drawn floor plan, build a 3D computer model and produce and publish a complete set of house plans. Working with the structural engineer, plan reviewer and contractor is covered, as well. The entire process can be accomplished on a home computer with free software available on the internet saving thousands of dollars. The focus here is on the innovative Monolithic dome, but the method described will work for any style of construction. A companion website provides additional information, links and color versions of many of the images found in the book. Foreword by David South, Pres. Monolithic Dome Institute.

Pick up a copy on amazon.com.

The Planar Head Workbook is also available as a Kindle book on amazon.com.

COMING SOON

Disaster strikes a family in the mid-west when a tornado takes everything but their lives. They vow never again will they be so vulnerable and exposed to the raw forces of nature. They begin to ask questions. Why do people continue to build houses that fly apart in a tornado offering no protection to life and property? Is there another way? The answers they find my surprise you. (Spoiler: there is another way!)

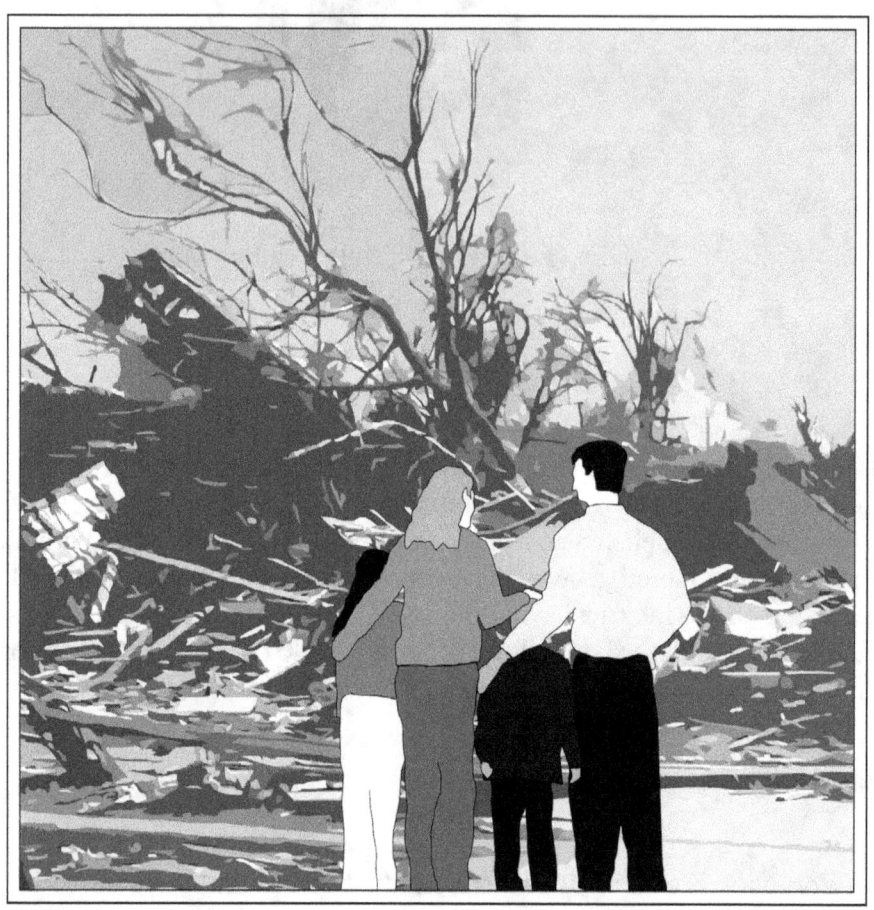

Never Again
by Robert Bissett